GOD THE FATHER

The Divine Mother Of All Who Love Him

B.J.Wittrock

ISBN-13: 979-8-9948189-4-7 (PB)
ISBN-13: 979-8-9948189-6-1 (EPUB)

Printed in the United States of America

To God Be All The Glory

CONTENTS

INTRODUCTION

Merely, by His grace, do I stand before the Lord our God with the means to write. Such writings that would allow me to speak to the Word of God; insomuch that He is the One to be honored, praised, worshiped, exalted, magnified, and glorified in all things and by all things. Now and forevermore. I came to write this book not of my own accord but after several years of having ephemeral yet poignant coercions that had been slowly cultivating from within my heart. Eventually, the compulsions became too strong to ignore; therefore, I began to pray to the Lord, asking for further discernment and guidance. I wanted to know with certainty that what I was feeling compelled to write was truly coming from the Holy Spirit, and not from elsewhere. As I continued to seek guidance from the Lord, I became more and more encouraged and strengthened to write. Though at the time I wasn't sure what was to come of it, and neither did I know that it might become a book.

Several years ago, through manifold experiences, it was brought to my attention that there are countless people who actively disregard God, Christianity, and the Bible itself, merely because of the 5th commandment. Upon learning this, I felt compelled to further research, ponder, and pray, in the hopes that I could write something that would not only bring glory to God but also in the hopes of leading people to Jesus, and not away. As it were, for the deep grief and sorrow that I have for humanity, is what further compelled me to write; as I have come to witness and experience the multitudes of children and adults who suffer and struggle to survive spiritually within this world. But not only spiritually—psychologically, physiologically, and sociologically. Millions of people ask every day, why is there so much suffering in this world? My quick and short answer is this: I exhort you to read the Bible, which will provide you with a good understanding of your question. However, in many ways, only God has the ultimate answer to this question. But then again, in many ways, the answer is right before us as we do not have to look far to see the forest through the trees. Might it just be that we as free agents through our God-given free will—having the ability to do as we choose—have essentially brought devastation upon ourselves through ongoing disobedience and ignorance? Disregarding God's 5th commandment along with His many other commandments; as humanity perpetually endeavors to maintain control and not surrender to God. Might it just be that at some point long ago, the 5th commandment like many other aspects of this world, was adulterated and distorted from its original context in order to lead humanity astray? Which by no means is uncommon; look at God's final commandment to us all, which is to love the Lord your God with all your heart, soul, mind, and strength, and to love others as you love yourself. This final commandment, even more so today, is profoundly disregarded. And as it is with love, honor has also been disregarded and denigrated. In Hebrew, the word "honor" is translated to Kavod: this definition is comprised of social, moral, and theological implications that are derived from the Hebrew root word for "weight" - which is to honor, to respect, to revere, to show importance, to distinguish, to dignify, to look up to, to venerate, or even to glorify. My objective here is to make known that God the Father is the One who is to be honored and glorified in all things as being the Ultimate Father and Mother—that He is the only One, who is everlasting. When we choose to put God first in our lives, we discover through Him how to faithfully love and honor Him and others as well.

GOD THE FATHER IS WHO WE ARE TO HONOR IN THE 5TH COMMANDMENT

Ephesians 1:4-5
"Even as he chose us in him before the foundation of the world, that we should be holy and blameless before him. In love he predestined us for adoption to himself as sons through Jesus Christ, according to the purpose of his will, to the praise of his glorious grace, with which he has blessed us in the Beloved."

In the garden of Eden, if God had handed Adam and Eve the 10 commandments—which He very well could have—who would be the father and mother they are to honor within the 5th commandment? In the beginning, as it was with Adam and Eve, so it was with Moses and the rest of humanity; we were all created by the same Father and under the same commandments—including the 5th commandment. So my question remains: Why is it that nearly every theological commentator who is about to address the topic or give a message on the 5th commandment begins their message with saying something like this: "For many of you, this topic can be challenging and is a difficult one to address; however, let's work through it together so that we can understand the meaning behind the 5th commandment." Could it be that, perhaps, there is a justifiable reason for why this topic is so challenging for so many people? Why is it that the 5th commandment is the cause of so much apprehension to the spirit of many Christians and even non-Christians? Aren't we called by God to honor everyone? Perhaps, could it be that the 5th commandment from its inception, like many other commandments of God, had become adulterated and distorted as it was passed down from posterity to posterity?:

2 Peter 3:16

"Speaking of this as he does in all his letters. There are some things in them hard to understand, which the ignorant and unstable twist to their own destruction, as they do the other Scriptures."

What evidence is there, and why is it automatically and even unconsciously assumed that the 5th commandment pertains to earthly fathers and mothers? What basis is this perpetual assumption founded upon? Why do people have such difficulty conceptualizing the premise that it is God Himself who is the Father and Mother spoken of in the 5th commandment? Why does this concept strike such a nerve with so many? —especially those who are parents. Is it because the concept is unbiblical? —likely not. If it were unbiblical, then explain how it is that the entire corpus of the Bible points to Jesus Christ (God) as Creator, Savior, Father, and through many words describes Him as being the ultimate divine Mother. To me, it just simply makes sense; knowing that we were all created in His likeness and image (Genesis 1:26-27), being that all masculinity and femininity is derived from God Himself. Could it be that the devil, as he attempts to do with all God's commandments, has distorted, twisted, and manipulated the 5th commandment and its true meaning—and we bought into it? Or perhaps could it be that the naturally conceited hostile heart in humanity wants it to be about them and not God? Consider this: of all people, Moses, the man to whom God first handed the ten commandments, had never known his parents personally other than when he was born as an infant. Was this just coincidental? Of course not, nothing is coincidental with God. Thus, when God handed the tablets of the ten commandments to Moses—God's chosen leader—do you suppose the first thing Moses said in question to God upon reading the 5th commandment was "You want me to honor my father and mother? How am I supposed to do that when I don't even know who they are and have never met them, aside from when I was an infant?" Likely not, and if I had to guess, Moses probably did not even bat an eye at the 5th commandment or any of the others for that matter. Because Moses knew without any further thought that the father and mother spoken of in the 5th commandment were God Himself. Moses knew that he and the Israelites were children of the Most High God. Likewise, the Israelites, who upon receiving the 10 commandments, also did not think twice about who the 5th commandment was referring to—they knew that the Father and Mother whom they were to honor was God Himself. And despite the Israelites receiving these commandments from God, it wasn't too long after that they quickly disregarded the 5th commandment and the others, as they turned to worship false idols and false gods. Moreover, amid the Israelites worshiping these false idols and gods, they conspicuously twisted and distorted God's commandments along with the 5th and did so for their own self-serving reasons. Moreover, as the 10 commandments were passed down from posterity to posterity, the Israelites took the 5th commandment and made it about them and not God; just as they had done with the other commandments:

Psalm 78:56-58

"Yet they tested and rebelled against the Most High God and did not keep his testimonies, but turned away and acted treacherously like their fathers; they twisted like a deceitful bow. For they provoked him to anger with their high places; they moved him to jealousy with their idols."

I am delving into this chapter vociferously and even tempestuously, as I attempt to dissolve any emotional schemes that may arise and come to thought as the devil through deception endeavors to diminish the true power and meaning behind the 5th commandment. So, before you continue to believe any further through conventional ideology that God gave the 5th commandment merely to children and/or adult children—that they are to "Honor your father and mother" (their parents here on Earth) —I ask that you first take into account all of what you are about to read. So, without further delay, I dare you to tell the following children to "Honor their earthly father and mother": Tell this to the child who has been beaten and raped by their own earthly father or mother. Tell this to the child who has been sold by a parent to human trafficking. Tell this to the child who has been sold to a pimp—to become a prostitute—so the child's mother or father could get their "fix" (drugs) for the day. Tell this to the child who was physically beaten and tortured by their father and/or mother. Tell this to the child who grew up in foster homes throughout childhood, as they were tossed around like an object of no worth. Tell this to the child who early on in life had been abandoned or rejected by their father and/or mother. Tell this to the child who has been manipulated, lied to, and betrayed their entire life by their parents. Tell this to the child who was born into this world from the womb with various types of recreational drugs in their system because the mother was a drug addict, and so now the child is an addict. Tell this to the child who does not know who their father is; because even the mother herself is not certain who the father is because she had slept around most of her life. Tell this to the child who grew up having parents who for all intents and purposes sought to destroy each other and their children through emotional and physical abuse. Tell this to the child who was never told by their father or mother that they are loved. Tell this to the child who throughout their childhood was taught by their parents how to manipulate and exploit others, but then as an adult learned and realized what was happening. This list touches only the surface of what has all occurred amongst parents and children; and the majority of children and/or adult-children can in some manner relate to one or more of these scenarios. So, tell me, who are these children supposed to honor? Their earthly father and mother? You see, while for some children and/or adult children it may seem natural for them to say, "oh sure, of course, honor your parents—obey the 5th commandment." However, for the majority, this concept is egregious, impractical, and even harrowing for the many children who have experienced the situations as described above. God the Father is a God of compassion, justice, righteousness, love, mercy, and grace; therefore, by no means does He expect a child or even an adult child who has gone through such experiences as described above, and command them to "honor their earthly father and mother." Many theologians in various ways have long attempted to rationalize the premise behind the 5th commandment. However, by doing so, many have oversimplified and have even dishonored God in the process. Oftentimes, we see many of the same verses or passages from within scripture used in an attempt to corroborate the definitive meaning behind the 5th commandment and how it supposedly relates to our earthly parents. Many commentators have even become apprehensive as they approach the threshold of opposing the idea that the 5th commandment was not meant specifically for children. But that in all actuality, it was intended more specifically for adults. Moreover, commentators will often choose the less contentious path in an attempt to avoid the reality that the 5th commandment has less to do with earthly parents, but everything to do with God Himself. They believe that if they keep things simple through conventional and political thinking, they won't have to worry about disrupting common ideology and theology, or even more so, the congregation. Many commentators, as they endeavor to stand behind their premise of the 5th commandment, will go on to say that if it weren't for the guidance of a child's parents, even from birth, the child would have likely been injured or harmed or would have even died. Which is utterly just not true and is narrow-minded to say the least. Even full-grown adults do not take their next breath unless God gives it and allows it. Look at the number of children over time who have been orphaned from an early age, tossed to the streets (literally), placed into dumpsters at birth, yet they survive. On a daily basis, many infants are left abandoned in various places, to maybe be found and cared for by others. Look at the countless number of children who, for all intents and purposes, have had their parents watching over them every waking hour of the day, yet something occurs and they die. These various types of events occur every day; we just don't always hear about them. So, you see, no child passes away from this earth without God knowing and allowing it to happen. If a parent were to forthrightly shove their 2-year-old toddler out the front door of their home and were to say to the toddler "good luck," that toddler is still entirely in the hands of the Lord. And as it were, with a plan already in place—though with tears in His eyes and with a sorrowful yet indignant heart—the Lord allowed the nefarious parent to shove that child out the front door. Look at the story of Moses; his parents—though not for nefarious reasons but for good—placed their infant child (Moses) into a basket and set him into the Nile River amongst some reeds, in order to hide the child. It's uncertain how long he was there, but was likely there for hours or maybe even days. Either way, it's clear that the Lord was watching over Moses and that He had a plan for him well before any of the events had ever taken place. So you see, again, nothing occurs outside of God's will; whether it be a child who is cared for by responsible parents or whether a child is in the care of irresponsible parents. The concept of God being in control of everything at all times seems so primitive to most; therefore, most people cannot or just simply do not want to come to terms with the fact that we have a God who functions well beyond our comprehension and understanding, knowing that He does so as an unconditionally loving Father (and Mother). Now, one might be asking, "Why does God first and foremost identify and address Himself as a Father and not so much as a mother if He is essentially both? And, how can He also be a mother if He is ultimately the Father?" The answer is really quite simple; because He is God. Look all around you—look up—look at His creation; therefore, cease from trying to comprehend what you cannot. God functions well beyond our understanding. Therefore, He does as He pleases and addresses Himself as He pleases;

which happens to be first and foremost as the Father and as a masculine-male figure. If you want to argue this further, take it up with God Himself. I assure you that He will in some manner answer you. And when He does, don't miss His answer, because He will respond in the most loving, merciful, and gracious way, because it is who He is. Wisdom (God's wisdom that is), tells us that within the realm of life there must be some sort of hierarchical structure, just as there is in all realms of life. Without hierarchical structures there is essentially no structure at all. And wherever there is no structure, it leaves only one thing: chaos, disorder, and destruction. Jesus Himself said, "A house divided will not stand." Look at the present condition of the world, a world where humanity is ignoring God and all His structures; a world where relativism, pluralism, and division are the "structures." We have a world where everyone seeks to live their own independent lives based on their own ideologies, with which there is no foundation or structure. Just because God's structure begins with masculinity does not mean He is without the qualities and characteristics of femininity. And though God first and foremost identifies and addresses Himself as being the ultimate Father, by no means do we want to attenuate His characteristics of motherhood. The mother figure is just as important as the father figure; remember, Jesus was born in flesh from a mother, that's profound. Thus, God the Father within whom He is also holds the position and title of being the ultimate divine Mother. In Matthew 12:46-50, Jesus makes it very clear that to Him there is no delineation among us as children of God other than that we are male and female; that's the delineation, that's the structure. Jesus is the structure; He is the hierarchy; He is the Head, and He shows no partiality. We belong to Him, we are His church body—we are all one body in Him—male and female. In the following passage you are about to read, as was spoken by Jesus, further shows that we are all one in Him and that there is no partiality amongst humanity here on Earth. But at the same time, Jesus is also making it clear that for those who belong to Him, we have only one Father (and essentially even one mother):

Matthew 12:46-50

"While he was still speaking to the people, behold, his mother and his brothers stood outside, asking to speak to him. But he replied to the man who told him, 'Who is my mother, and who are my brothers?' And stretching out his hand toward his disciples, he said, 'Here are my mother and my brothers! For whoever does the will of my Father in heaven is my brother and sister and mother.'"

Did you catch that? Jesus says, "Who is my mother?" Wouldn't this be dishonoring His earthly mother (Mary) and even His earthly father (Joseph) and even all other fathers and mothers here on Earth by saying these things? Wouldn't Jesus be breaking His own law and commandment; but even more so, the 5th commandment? Is Jesus a hypocrite for saying this? Of course not, what Jesus is saying here is quite profound if you can understand and let it resonate. Notice that Jesus does not include father in His line-up, which may be obvious as to why, but I will further expound on that here shortly. Jesus by no means is abasing anyone here by saying "Who is my mother and who are my brothers (and sisters)." What He is saying is that anyone and everyone who believes in Him and chooses to follow Him has become one with Him; one body, one church. He is the vine; we are the branches. Therefore, through Jesus, we become consecrated and sanctified by the shedding of His blood on the cross and through His resurrection. Death no longer has any hold on those who are in Christ Jesus. At the end of Matthew 12:46-50, Jesus says "For whoever does the will of my Father in heaven is my brother and sister and mother." Jesus is telling us that we who are God's spiritual children have no delineation of titles among us: such as father, mother, brother, or sister, not according to the way we perceive it here on Earth. We all are simply, yet profoundly, sons and daughters of the Most High God. Jesus does not list <u>father</u> as one of the identifiers among those who belong to Him. Why? Because Jesus is forthrightly elucidating that He and we (who are in Christ) have only one Father—God the Father. Furthermore, Jesus is conveying that He and we (who are of His church body), have no longer an earthly mother but an ultimate divine heavenly Mother (God) —Jesus said, "Who is my mother." Again, Jesus in what He said is not diminishing or dishonoring earthly mothers, after all, He was born in flesh by an earthly mother. However, Jesus also knows that mothers here on Earth are not divine, nor are they ultimate, and nor are they God—aside from the mere fact that not all mothers here on Earth are guaranteed and destined for the Kingdom of God. Matthew 15:1-9, which you are soon to read, irrefutably corroborates the premise that the 5th commandment is for God Himself and that He is the Father and Mother we are to honor within the 5th commandment. So, without delay, yet with discernment, let us read into Matthew 15:1-9 and here the words that Jesus spoke from within it:

Matthew 15:1-9

"Then Pharisees and scribes came to Jesus from Jerusalem and said, 'Why do your disciples break the tradition of the

elders?' 'For they do not wash their hands when they eat.' He answered them, 'And why do you break the commandment of God for the sake of your tradition?' 'For God commanded, 'Honor your father and your mother,' and whoever reviles father or mother must surely die.' 'But you say, if anyone tells his father or his mother, what you would have gained from me is given to God, he need not honor his father.' 'So, for the sake of your tradition, you have made void the word of God.' 'You hypocrites!' 'Well, did Isaiah prophesy of you, when he said: this people honors me with their lips, but their heart is far from me; in vain do they worship me, teaching as doctrines the commandments of men.'"

Did you catch that last sentence? If not, reread it. The last sentence could not be any more conspicuous in the fact that God is speaking of Himself as being the Father and Mother who the Pharisees are to be honoring within the 5th commandment (though they are not). Which is why Jesus said what He said. Let me also further point out that Jesus is speaking merely to a group of adults (the Pharisees), and not to children. He is speaking to the Pharisees and Scribes who hold fast so stringently to their own man-made laws and traditions that they have become blind and deaf to the real truth. Jesus is pointing out how they mislead and condemn others by their own man-made laws and beliefs while they themselves disregard the very commandments of God. And that while doing so, they also boast and take credit in their evil ways. The Pharisees through their own deception and pride are too blind to realize that they themselves are caught up in the very sin they preach about and is the very reason why Jesus calls them out as hypocrites. Jesus then goes on to say how the Pharisees and Scribes honor God with their lips (their words), but that their actions completely contradict their teachings and preachings. That their words are spoken in vain and are done so for their very own self-serving ambitions. But then Jesus makes another vociferous statement to the Pharisees; He says to them, "Whoever reviles father and mother must surely die." Which, by Him saying this, leaves no further question but only just affirms that God is the "father and mother" being spoken of in Matthew 15:4:

Matthew 15:4

"Whoever reviles father and mother must surely die."

Remember, it is Jesus speaking these words: "Whoever reviles father and mother must surely die" —not a third party. Therefore, let's be pragmatic and think logically here as we put this verse into context. Would God say to a child or even to an adult-child: "Whoever reviles father and mother must surely die," not plausible. Let me put it another way, would God say to a child or even to an adult-child (and I paraphrase): "If you revile your parents here on earth, I'm going to kill you," again, not plausible. Not only is this not plausible, but has there ever been a time where God had carried this out in scripture? No, but what we have seen is God act this out towards those who have reviled <u>Him</u>. Therefore, Matthew 15:4 "Whoever reviles father and mother must surely die," irrefutably speaks and refers to God Himself as being the Father and Mother and not to earthly parents. Furthermore, if Jesus in Matthew 15:4 spoke these words in relation to earthly fathers and mothers and was not referring to God Himself, then humanity would have become extinct long ago. Why, because all children and even adult-children have unequivocally at some point in their lifetime and in some manner reviled their earthly parents. Thus, if we apply Matthew 15:4 to all humanity—which we should—

then humanity, due to reviling, would have died off a long time ago. Furthermore, one could even make the case that it is more common for a parent to knowingly be reviling a child than it would be for a child to knowingly be reviling a parent. This can be said because most children—at least not until nearing adulthood—have the cognitive ability to understand what they are doing according to the word of God, much less what it even truly means to revile someone. Yes, of course, children can and will disagree and become angry or upset with their parents and others; however, for them to be wittingly reviling to its extent, is just not plausible. The word revile and the context in which it is being used here in Matthew 15:4 describes a person who is being verbally and emotionally abusive towards God and is likely attacking Him with evil, aggressive, and blasphemous words. Which is the very reason why Jesus forthrightly says, "Whoever reviles father and mother must surely die." Thus, leaving only one outcome for the one who rejects and reviles God—spiritual death—which is eternal death. Jesus said, for anyone who rejects Him—they will be rejected by the Father (God):

Matthew 10:32-33

"So, everyone who acknowledges me before men, I also will acknowledge before my Father who is in heaven, but whoever denies me before men, I also will deny before my Father who is in heaven."

Therefore, in the passage of Matthew 15:1-9, we see how it leaves no room for further question that Jesus was speaking to God Himself as being the Father and Mother within the passage. And that it is God who is the Father and Mother of the 5th commandment—as it is irrefutable that Jesus related everything of what He said in that passage to the 5th commandment. As we continue on into the book of Matthew and only within a few chapters later, Jesus further expounds on the fact that God, and only God, is to be regarded as the ultimate Father and that there is none other. Which, if God is the ultimate Father, then it only makes sense that there must be an ultimate mother figure, and He is it:

Matthew 23:9

"And call no man your father on earth, for you have one Father, who is in heaven."

It is often said by many commentators that this verse and the passage that surrounds it were spoken metaphorically and that it is not to be taken in a literal sense. My response to anyone who wants to depict or categorize this verse (which, let me remind you, are the words of Jesus) as a metaphor and not hold it to be literal is this: On that great day when Jesus comes in all His glory, I shrink back to even be a fly on the wall when any such person stands before God and says to Him, "Oh yes, when your Son Jesus said to 'Call no man here on earth your father, for you have one Father, who is in heaven'" and says to Jesus, "Yeah, what you said, that was merely just a metaphor." Once again, I, as a fly on the wall, upon hearing a person tell Jesus that what He said was a metaphor, would then go from being a fly on the wall to a fly on its knees begging for that person's mercy. There's no doubt that humanity likes to twist and distort things, but a person must be twisted themselves for them to want to twist what Jesus said about "calling no man here on earth your father, but that you have only one Father, who is in heaven," depicting it as a metaphor. Let us not forget that when God says something, He means it; which in this matter, He means it, literally. We see all too often how people will take scripture and will attempt to diminish it down to a metaphor just so they don't have to abide by its true meaning, especially if they don't understand the context in which it is being used and especially if it doesn't align with their views. While it is true that, throughout scripture, Jesus did often speak many things in parables and metaphorically, however, this was not one of those times. Jesus, throughout the New Testament, addresses God as "Father" more than any other way and does so for good reason. When you become a part of the body of Christ, you become a child of God; therefore, God the Father becomes your ultimate Father—with none other. While, yes, in a general or broad sense, God throughout the Old Testament and New Testament makes it clear that He ultimately is the Father of all creation, however, not all people become children of His eternal Heavenly Kingdom. However, if you have been born again in Christ Jesus, then you have only one Father, as you become His eternal child. But if you have not been born again in Christ Jesus and are living for this world and not for the Kingdom of God, then you have only earthly fathers (and mothers); which, let me remind you, they are not eternal. And if your earthly father and/or mother have accepted Jesus as Lord and Savior and are a part of the body of Christ, then for all intents and purposes, your earthly father and mother are no longer your father and mother anyways (as we saw earlier in Matthew 12:46-50). Yes, you still honor and love your parents just as you would anyone else here on Earth, but they are not your "was, and is, and is to come" —only God the Father is your "was, and is, and is to come." In Matthew 23:9 as you previously read, Jesus was admonishing the Pharisees because they were abusing and misrepresenting the symbolic title of father; therefore, they were dishonoring God and glorifying themselves, and that is why Jesus spoke what He did. If we appropriate what Jesus said in Matthew 23:9 "And call no man your father on earth, for you have one Father, who is in heaven" and assimilate the characteristics of the Pharisees to those of modern-time clergymen, we see why Jesus spoke what He did. For example: we have men of the clergy and of various religions who forthrightly address themselves as "fathers" and as "priests" as they attempt to distinguish or segregate themselves from all other people—people who are otherwise of the church body (the body of Christ). They justify themselves and their actions in the premise that they are some type of "special spiritual fathers and priests called by God." However, much like the Pharisees, they often have their own man-made precepts and agendas that are unbiblical. God foreknew and foresaw how, not only the Pharisees, but humanity itself would abuse, twist, and pervert the titles of fatherhood and priesthood by using them for their own propaganda. It's no wonder Jesus said in Matthew 23:9 "Call no man here on earth your father" —and is likely one of several reasons as to why God commanded that Jesus is the High Priest forever—in spirit and carnally:

Hebrews 7:17

"For it is witnessed of him, 'You are a priest forever, after the order of Melchizedek.'"

Psalm 110:4

"The LORD has sworn and will not change his mind, 'You are a priest forever after the order of Melchizedek.'"

Which, for all intents and purposes, Jesus had already been the forever High Priest and was so even before Jesus became High Priest carnally here on Earth. Scripture expressly states that all children of God—those who are of

the body of Christ—are a "royal priesthood":
1 Peter 2:9
"But you are a chosen race, a royal priesthood, a holy nation, a people for his own possession, that you may proclaim the excellencies of him who called you out of darkness into his marvelous light."
Within the New Testament, Ephesians 6:1-4, written by the Apostle Paul, is often a default passage with which most every commentator looks to in their attempt to vindicate the 5th commandment as it relates to children or adult-children and their parents here on Earth:
Ephesians 6:1-4
"Children, obey your parents in the Lord, for this is right. 'Honor your father and mother,' which is the first commandment with promise: 'that it may be well with you and you may live long on the earth.' And you, fathers, do not provoke your children to wrath, but bring them up in the training and admonition of the Lord."
My intent here as I walk through this passage is to impart full honor to God as I endeavor to unpack its meaning and purpose. First, let's recall who the Apostle Paul was writing this letter to: the church of Ephesus. Paul wrote and began his letter by saying, "To the Saints who are in Ephesus and are faithful in Christ Jesus." Thus, alluding to the fact that these people are God-fearing Christians who strive to abide in God, His Word, and in His given 10 commandments. With one of the commandments being, of course, the 5th commandment—which is to "Honor your father and mother." Now, beginning with the first verse (Ephesians 6:1) of this passage, Paul says: "Children, obey your parents in the Lord, for this is right." Paul in Ephesians 6:2 then goes on to say, "Honor your father and mother." This is where commentators automatically

assume and will associate Ephesians 6:1 with Ephesians 6:2 (“obey your parents—honor your father and mother”) as if the two verses are speaking to the same persons. Though, Paul is not. As we see, Paul wrote “Honor your father and mother” in quotations; and did so to show us that he was quoting the 5th commandment. Thus, Paul is insinuating and assumes that both adults and children of the Ephesus church have been taught the 5th commandment according to its original context in which it was given—in the sense that God is the “Father and Mother” who they all are to honor. Which is why Paul starts off the passage by telling the children of the church to obey their parents, that by doing so they will be honoring not only their parents in the process but ultimately God the Father (and Mother) of the 5th commandment. Paul then goes on to say, “This is the first commandment with a promise.” Why does Paul say this? Paul is again quoting scripture and is reiterating one of God’s previously spoken commandments, which was given to Moses and then proclaimed to the Israelites:

Deuteronomy 4:40

“Thou shalt keep therefore his statutes, and his commandments, which I command thee this day, that it may go well with thee, and with thy children after thee, and that thou mayest prolong thy days upon the earth, which the LORD thy God giveth thee, for ever.”

Did you catch what was said at the end of Deuteronomy 4:40? —which says, “and that thou mayest prolong thy days upon the earth, which the LORD thy God giveth thee, for ever.” “For ever” —in other words, for eternity. This means only one thing, which tells us that Moses was speaking to the Kingdom of God and not of this present earth; but of the new heaven and of the new earth. Thus, it is why in Ephesians 6:3 Paul then goes on to say (as he quotes Moses), "that it may be well with you and you may live long on the earth." This further shows us that in the grand scheme of things, Paul is speaking not to the children of the church but more specifically to the adults—the parents and even the leaders and elders of the church. Because Paul knows that it is the responsibility of the elders, the leaders, but even more so the parents of the church, who are to be teaching their children the commandments of God. Which includes the 5th commandment; to "Honor your father and mother" —God. Furthermore, do you think Paul is going to place such an expectation and/or burden on the children of Ephesus in the idea that if they don't obey their parents "that it won't go well with them and that they won't live long in the land that God is to give them," not plausible. Consider this: did God say to Isaac (who was also a child at the time), "Now Isaac, obey your father, Abraham; as he is about to offer you up as a sacrifice to Me, because if you don't, things won't go well with you." No, God did not say such a thing and neither did Paul say this to the children of Ephesus. Nevertheless, Paul was already having much of a difficult time compelling the many adults of the church to obey and abide by the commandments of God. Therefore, it would be foolish of Paul to expect more from the children when the children's parents can't even follow the rules. Furthermore, throughout Scripture, we often see how God does not let the sinful nature and actions of many parents dictate the final outcome and lives of their children. Jesus Himself, born in flesh, was of the lineage of many sinful posterities, which shows us that despite our ancestry, we can still become a child of the Most-High God and live a fruitful life. Finally, in Ephesians 6:4, Paul says, "And you, fathers, do not provoke your children to wrath, but bring them up in the training and admonition of the Lord." Notice, Paul does not say to the fathers that they are to "bring them up in the training and admonition of their parents," no, Paul says—of the Lord. Along with the fact that Paul is actually admonishing the "fathers" in what he spoke. Which further corroborates the fact that Paul was speaking to the adults of the church when he quoted to "Honor your father and mother." Paul's expectation here is that the fathers are to teach their children to adhere to the "discipline and instructions of the Lord" —which is precisely what Paul had been saying all along through the entire passage and even up to this final verse of the passage. Paul is telling the fathers of the church that it is their duty that they teach their children to first and foremost honor God (the Father and Mother) through discipline and instruction. Whereas, if the father provokes his children to anger through exploitation such as emotional and/or physical abuse, the father is demonstrating that he does not respect them or God. Moreover, not only will the children lose respect for their earthly father but will be hard-pressed to want to respect anyone else going forward—including God the Father—the ultimate Father. Because if children cannot even trust their father and/or mother here on earth, who can they trust? We see the manifestations of this mistrust occurring at a catastrophic rate within the lives of so many children and adult-children today. And is all the more reason why the 5th commandment was given to adult fathers and mothers who then are to teach and instruct their children how to honor the eternal and ultimate Father and Mother—God. Remember, earthly fathers and mothers are not guaranteed to be around for another minute, and neither are they assured to enter the Kingdom of God; not unless they have Jesus Christ in their hearts. Which further affirms that parents here on earth are merely stewards and that God the Father is the ultimate Father and Mother and is who children are to be fully relying upon. Even then, once parents and children leave this earth and enter into the kingdom of Heaven, parents are no longer parents but are children themselves of the Most-High God. Furthermore, what parent here on earth can say that they are “The beginning and the end” — “The first and the last” — “The alpha and the omega?” Here is my overall rendition of what Paul was conveying to the church of Ephesus (Ephesians 6:1-4); and I paraphrase: (Ephesians 6:1) “Children obey your parents in the Lord, for by doing so, you will ultimately be honoring God and His commandment. Because as we know, God is the ultimate Father and Mother of us all and is who we are to honor for eternity. (Ephesians 6:2) So, therefore, ‘Honor your Father and Mother’ (God) —just as He commanded long ago. And I, Paul, am commanding a promise given by the Lord; (Ephesians 6:3) which is, that the Lord will always work all things together for your good and for His glory because you love Him and He loves you. And though you will endure many hardships, trials, and tribulations here on Earth, know that the Lord your God will never leave you nor forsake you—and that He has a Kingdom that awaits you. (Ephesians 6:4) Fathers, do not provoke your children to anger lest they become angry at you and God. Causing them to not only turn away from you, but also from God. Because if your children can’t trust their father or mother here on Earth, they will have a difficult time trusting anyone else—including God. Therefore, fathers, teach your children the commandments of God and what it means to be a Christian; striving daily to obey and honor God—the ultimate Father and Mother of all Christians":

Psalm 78:5-8

"He established a testimony in Jacob and appointed a law in Israel, which he commanded our fathers to teach to their children, that the next generation might know them, the children yet unborn and arise and tell them to their children, so that they should set their hope in God and not forget the works of God, but keep his commandments; and that they should not be like their fathers, a stubborn and rebellious generation, a generation whose heart was not steadfast, whose spirit was not faithful to God."

Continuing on, to another passage that commentators often turn to as they attempt to relate the 5th commandment to parents here on Earth and not God Himself, is Exodus 20:12. However, in order for us to understand the meaning and purpose behind Exodus 20:12, it is important to hear what God has to say in the passage of Exodus 20:1-6 which precedes Exodus 20:12:

Exodus 20:1-6

"And God spoke all these words, saying, 'I am the Lord your God, who brought you out of the land of Egypt, out of the house of slavery. You shall have no other gods before me. You shall not make for yourself a carved image, or any likeness of anything that is in heaven above, or that is in the earth beneath, or that is in the water under the earth. You shall not bow down to them or serve them, for I the Lord your God am a jealous God, visiting the iniquity of the fathers on the children to the third and the fourth generation of those who hate me, but showing steadfast love to thousands of those who love me and keep my commandments.'"

Exodus 20:12

"Honor your father and your mother, that your days may be long in the land that the Lord your God is giving you."

First, let me once again point out that in these verses God was unequivocally speaking these commandments to the adult Israelites, and not to children. Thus, as we dissect the meaning behind Exodus 20:12 and the entire passage surrounding it, let us again use discernment as we look to the bigger picture and take all things into account. In Exodus 20:1-6 God says that "He is a jealous God"; He says to "not make any graven images, nor to serve or to make any other thing (including humans) an object of idolization before God Himself." God then forthrightly goes on to say that the fathers of the children of that generation are filled with iniquity: i.e. wickedness, sinfulness, immorality, and evil, but that He intends to show mercy upon the generations to follow—more specifically to those who love Him and keep His commandments. That said, Exodus 20:12 is without doubt referring to God Himself as being the Father and Mother who is to be obeyed. If God were not specifically referring to Himself in Exodus 20:12, God would otherwise be contradicting Himself, and here is why. We know with certainty that God is not going to point out and call out the iniquity (wickedness, sinfulness, immorality, evil, etc.) of the fathers of that generation, but then within only a few sentences later is God then going to command children and/or adult-children to "Honor your father and mother, that your days may be long in the land that the Lord your God is giving you." That said, it would be utterly counter-intuitive and even hypocritical of God to on one hand state how wicked and evil the fathers are, but to then turn around and tell children and/or adult-children to "Honor your father and mother." Furthermore, as was pointed out earlier in Deuteronomy, if we apply Exodus 20:12 to this present day: which says, "that your days may be long in the land that the Lord your God is giving you"; we know that the land to which it speaks, is the Kingdom of God—our eternal home. So you see, and as it pertains to Exodus 20:12; parents here on Earth can promise children all they want, but unless God gives it and provides it, parents have nothing to give. Because without God, parents, upon their own volition, have nothing—and is all the more reason why God is to be glorified in everything and for everything:

John 3:27

"A person cannot receive even one thing unless it is given him from heaven."

James 1:16-17

"Do not be deceived, my beloved brothers. Every good gift and every perfect gift is from above, coming down from the Father of lights, with whom there is no variation or shadow due to change."

Now, let's turn to Wisdom and the Book of Wisdom to help us further corroborate the true meaning and purpose behind the 5th commandment—as it was given by God and for His glory. First, I should point out to you that all throughout the Book of Proverbs there are many verses that speak and refer to a "father" and "mother." This "father" and "mother" is oftentimes God Himself—God being the Father of course but also being the mother—"Mother Wisdom." However, at times the author does also refer and speak to earthly fathers and mothers as well. If you pay close attention, you will see when the author is speaking to mothers and fathers of the Earth versus to God Himself. Once you read the book of Proverbs with an open mind, you will begin to see the delineation; it just might take a few times of reading it. But for now, I am going to provide you with verses that unequivocally show and point to God as being the father and mother to which they speak. I also hope for you to see within these verses how God reiterates the importance of not only what it means to honor Him, but how we are to honor Him through His wisdom and teachings as we live out our lives for Him and through Him:

Proverbs 1:20

"Wisdom (Mother) cries aloud in the street, in the markets she raises her voice."

Proverbs 2:6

"For the LORD gives wisdom; from his mouth come knowledge and understanding."

Proverbs 1:8

"Hear, my son, your father's (God's) instruction, and forsake not your mother's (Wisdom) teaching."

Proverbs 10:1

"A wise son makes a glad father (God), but a foolish son is a sorrow to his mother (Wisdom)."

Proverbs 6:20

"My son, keep your father's (God's) commandment, and forsake not your mother's (Wisdom's) teaching."

Proverbs 15:20

"A wise son makes a glad father (God), but a foolish man despises his mother (Wisdom)."

Proverbs 4:1-13

"Hear, O sons, a father's instruction, and be attentive, that you may gain insight, for I give you good precepts; do not forsake my teaching. When I was a son with my father, tender, the only one in the sight of my mother, he taught me and said to me, 'Let your heart hold fast my words; keep my commandments, and live.' Get wisdom; get insight; do not forget, and do not turn away from the words of my mouth. Do not

forsake her (Wisdom), and she will keep you; love her, and she will guard you. The beginning of wisdom is this: Get wisdom, and whatever you get, get insight. Prize her highly, and she will exalt you; she will honor you if you embrace her. She will place on your head a graceful garland; she will bestow on you a beautiful crown.' Hear, my son, and accept my words, that the years of your life may be many. I have taught you the way of wisdom; I have led you in the paths of uprightness. When you walk, your step will not be hampered, and if you run, you will not stumble. Keep hold of instruction; do not let go; guard her, for she is your life."

Proverbs 23:22, as you will soon read below, assimilates Proverbs 15:20 (one of the verses you just read), and is another verse that has been used by commentators in an attempt to coerce the reader into conforming to the premise that the 5th commandment relates to earthly parents and not God Himself. However, if we take all things into account along with wisdom being our guide, we can discover the truth to which it speaks:

Proverbs 23:22

"Listen to your father (God), who gave you life, and do not despise your mother (Wisdom) when she is old."

Upon reading this verse, right away we see that it irrefutably speaks to our heavenly Father; knowing that He is the One who ultimately gave us life. Because, surely, it wasn't our earthly father who "bore" us into this world and gave us life. Furthermore, (fleshly speaking) if anyone birthed us into this world, it would have been our earthly mother and not our father. Therefore, this is our first indication that this verse speaks to God the Father and not to our earthly parents. Moreover, if this verse were relating to our earthly parents, wouldn't it make more sense for it to otherwise say: "Listen to your mother who gave you life, and do not despise your father when he gets old?" Thus, Proverbs 23:22 just as it states, is correct; as it speaks to our heavenly Father "who birthed us" (in spirit) and to our heavenly Mother (God) who gives us wisdom—and is why we are to "not despise your mother when she is old." Oftentimes, as we get older, we in our pride, arrogance, and conceitedness will begin to believe that we essentially have become wiser than wisdom (God) itself. Which is why we are to "not despise wisdom when she gets old" — (humanly speaking) old to us that is. I once heard a woman at the age of around 60 years, who not only proclaimed to be a Christian but was a mother, nonetheless; who upon being confronted about her sinful and prideful ways, sneered as she made this statement: "I'm old enough now, I can do whatever I want." This would be a prime example of someone who for all intents and purposes as she had grown older, had become "wise" in her own eyes— "despising her Mother" (Wisdom). Rebelling against God with a spirit of conceitedness and arrogance:

Ecclesiastes 4:13

"Better was a poor and wise youth than an old and foolish king who no longer knew how to take advice."

This woman's heart is desperately sick; she desperately needs Jesus and His wisdom, and not her own "wisdom":

Jeremiah 17:9-10

"The heart is deceitful above all things, and desperately sick; who can understand it? 'I the LORD search the heart and test the mind, to give every man according to his ways, according to the fruit of his deeds.'"

Paralleling Proverbs 23:22 is Proverbs 20:20. Which further shows that it only makes practical and logical sense that both of these verses refer to God as being the father and mother to whom they speak:

Proverbs 20:20

"If one curses his father or his mother, his lamp will be put out in utter darkness."

So you see, it is without doubt that God is the father and mother being spoken of in this verse, and the lamp is the Holy Spirit. How do we know? We know because Jesus Christ Himself said that He is the Lamp—the "Light of the World," and the Light that dwells within those who love Him. Furthermore, we know that only Jesus Himself (not anyone else, nor our parents) has the authority to impart to us or to take from us the Holy Spirit (The Lamp). God makes it very clear that whoever curses the Holy Spirit (Him only, not our earthly parents) will be rejected and not forgiven:

Matthew 12:31

"So I tell you, every sin and blasphemy can be forgiven—except blasphemy against the Holy Spirit, which will never be forgiven."

That said, this verse completely nullifies any premise that Proverbs 20:20 refers to earthly fathers and mothers but that it merely speaks to God Himself. Furthermore, we know unequivocally that throughout time many children and adult-children have in some manner and at some point have cursed their earthly father and mother. Thus, if Proverbs 20:20 was truly speaking to earthly fathers and mothers, then all of humanity would have been "put out in utter darkness" long ago; therefore, humanity would have already been nonexistent. From the book of Luke and 1 Corinthians, we see how both authors further corroborate that it is Jesus from whom Wisdom is ultimately derived—and that Jesus Himself is Wisdom—and is He who is justified by all her children (His church

body):
Luke 7:35
"Yet wisdom (Jesus) is justified by all her children (the church)."
1 Corinthians 1:30
"And because of him (God) you are in Christ Jesus, who became to us wisdom (Jesus) from God, righteousness and sanctification and redemption."
Let me finish the chapter by saying this: if you have yet to experience the profound yet incomprehensible love of God the Father, then you will have a difficult time appropriating and applying the premise that God the Father is the father and mother spoken of within the 5th commandment. However, if you have experienced the profound yet incomprehensible love of God the Father, then it is natural for you to see that God the Father is the father and mother of the 5th commandment and of all who love Him. We know that everything of what has been created and of what continues to be created, is made to point directly to God Himself and for His glory. Therefore, "Honor your father and mother" —your Creator and your God.
1 Corinthians 8:6
"But for us, there is one God, the Father, by whom all things were created, and for whom we live. And there is one Lord, Jesus Christ, through whom all things were created, and through whom we live."

WISDOM AND TRUTH CAN ONLY BE ATTAINED THROUGH A RELATIONSHIP WITH JESUS CHRIST

1 Corinthians 3:18-20

Stop deceiving yourselves. If you think you are wise by this world's standards, you need to become a fool to be truly wise. For the wisdom of this world is foolishness to God. As the Scriptures say, "He traps the wise in the snare of their own cleverness." And again, "The Lord knows the thoughts of the wise; he knows they are worthless."

You see, there is worldly wisdom, for which God says is futile and folly and is what leads to death; but then there is His wisdom, that which leads to life. So, you ask, what is wisdom and where does it come from? Well, as you just read in the passage, wisdom comes from He who is wisdom; however, let me further expound. Most people perceive wisdom and knowledge as being one and the same, though it is not. Most people perceive wisdom as something a person obtains through their years of experiences in living life within this world, though it is not. Many people perceive wisdom as something they have obtained upon reaching certain milestones, which is often based on their own perceptions, ideologies, and beliefs—which is incorrect and is narrow-mindedness, ignorance, and pride. Many also perceive wisdom as something they have "earned" upon "mastering" a skill, whether it be vocationally or in some other area of life. Now, let me provide you with further insight as to what wisdom truly is according to the Word of God: wisdom is when a person can accept the truth and reality that they actually lack wisdom, when in fact, they know very little. Not only would this be the beginning of wisdom but is also the beginning of knowledge—which opens the door to true Wisdom and Knowledge:

Proverbs 9:10

"The fear of the Lord is the beginning of wisdom, and knowledge of the Holy One is understanding."

As you read on, I hope for God to reveal to you further wisdom—His wisdom, which can only be obtained through having an intimate relationship with Jesus Christ. Because from God comes wisdom, and from wisdom comes humility, and from humility comes wisdom. I, like many, once thought I was wise, but then I met Jesus; realizing, I was a fool. So, let's appropriate the wisdom that comes only from God the Father and use it to glorify and honor Him. I want to begin this chapter by endeavoring to make known how the 5th commandment—like all the others—has always been about God, and not us. As we often see, much like most information that gets passed down from one person to the next or from one posterity to the next, the further it gets disseminated, the further it becomes dissected outside of its original context. Thus, the more likely it is to become distorted, diluted, and falsified along the way. Amongst most commentators, the debate continues; while they speculate as to why the 5th commandment has associated the first four commandments and why the 5th commandment, which is not directly related to God, was placed on the first tablet with the first four commandments. The answer is rather quite conspicuous; I can tell you with certainty that it was not by accident nor was it coincidental that God placed the 5th commandment to parallel the first four. Because let's be honest, in all reality, God could have made the 5th commandment to state many other important things. Such as (which would be fitting especially for that time), "Thou shall honor Moses" for being the leader and intermediary prophet through which the prescription of these commandments were given and is the one who led God's people out of slavery. However, God did not, because had He done so, God knew very well that people would go so far as to worship Moses in place of Him. But, even as we know, the Israelites turned to worship other idols anyway; such as a calf made of gold. God is very astute to the premise of how easily people worship false idols and even themselves, which is why God specifically categorized the 5th commandment to parallel the first four—because it's all about Him and not us. Thus, the 5th commandment was meant specifically for God Himself, and not earthly fathers and mothers. You see, God, if He desired, could have made the 5th commandment to say "Parents honor your children," however, He did not. Neither did God say, "Children honor your parents." One could easily make the argument that if God had a choice between "Children honor your father and mother" versus "Parents honor your children," I think it would be quite reasonable to say that most people would choose the latter of the two, and rightfully so. How so, you ask? Because as we know, children in comparison to adults are unequivocally the most vulnerable to exploitation, especially by their parents—not the other way around. Therefore, rationally and logically, it is for this reason, amongst many others, why the 5th commandment was given to adults; in the fact that adults first and foremost, along with their children, are to honor God—the Father and Mother. Because adults are the ones who are pre-supposed to have a mature, fully developed, competent, and rational state of mind. Furthermore, let us not forget who the commandments were imparted to in the first place; they were given to God's people, the Israelites—grown adults who were parents nonetheless, and many of them. The fact of the matter is there are many readers, commentators, and speculators who are parents themselves, who relish in the thought that God would even create a commandment that specifically identifies and speaks to them directly as "fathers and mothers." Therefore, we unequivocally have many parents who will in an unhealthy manner hold the 5th commandment over their child's head—just as a tyrant would. Whether society wants to acknowledge this or not is one thing, but it is certain that this type of behavior has occurred throughout history and is still very prevalent to this day. Thus, for many children and/or adult children, the premise of honoring their earthly father and/or mother is a lifelong painful process of spiritual, emotional, and even physical torment as their past haunts them for the duration of their time here on Earth. Moreover, many children cannot even begin to bear the idea of honoring their earthly father and/or mother without causing themselves further emotional trauma, even as adults. God, knowing preemptively that many horrible things would take place amongst parents and children here on Earth, forthrightly gave the 5th commandment in the hopes that there would be more God-fearing parents who, through wisdom, would adhere to His commandment of "Honoring your Father and Mother" (God):

James 3:13-18

"Who is wise and knowledgeable among you? Show by your good life that your works are done with gentleness born of wisdom. But if you have bitter envy and selfish ambition in

your hearts, do not be arrogant and lie about the truth. This is not wisdom that comes down from above but is earthly, unspiritual, demonic. For where there is envy and selfish ambition, there will also be disorder and wickedness of every kind. But the wisdom from above is first pure, then peaceable, gentle, willing to yield, full of mercy and good fruits, without a trace of partiality or hypocrisy. And the fruit of righteousness is sown in peace by those who make peace."

If we segregate the 5th commandment to its most commonly construed context in which it is often perceived, that it pertains to earthly parents, I then want to use wisdom along with some unconventional thinking to show you what it can truly mean for a child to "Honor their earthly father and mother" (their parents). Let's say that we have a child that is of a mature age cognitively; thus, the child is nearing the age of moving away from or has already moved out from living within their parents' home. Therefore, the child is soon to be or is no longer under the control of their parents' rules and/or regulations. And upon leaving their parents' home and even before moving out, this child has lived a God-like life by following and walking with Christ Jesus to the best of their ability as a Christian. However, the parents, on the other hand, have been living in a state of perpetual sin—never repenting, never acknowledging their sin, nor ever apologizing for any wrongdoing as they live in perpetual denial of who they are without any introspection. And though the parents claim to be "Christians," even attending church services every week, they otherwise are very much like the Pharisees and Sadducees of the Bible. In the sense that they do not practice what they preach; they are hypocrites. Often passing judgment and condemning just about anyone they can and for any given reason, and will do so for their own self-preservation; they point out the speck in other people's eyes, but have yet to remove the plank from within their own eye. In this given situation, the most honorable thing this child can do for his or her parents is to confront the parents on their perpetual sin; thus, by doing so, the child will be "honoring their father and mother." Whereas, if the child does not confront the parents on their sin, knowing that they stand condemned in their sin without repentance, one could say that the child is "dishonoring their father and mother" in ignorance. However, let's be wise, merciful, and gracious towards this child/adult-child as we consider all things and take all things into account. Because, depending on the child's situation, the idea of confronting their parents about their sin is likely no easy task and could lead to abuse or further abuse from the parents. Because many children who come from a household where sin is prevalent and perpetual, are already so oppressed by their tyrannical abusive parents that they cannot even begin to face the idea of confronting their parents about their sin. In many situations, the child fears for their life knowing that if they were to confront their parents it would likely elicit further abuse, or in some cases, even death. Moreover, and sadly, many of these children are already fighting for their lives from being so emotionally wounded that they have already begun to slowly die inside—spiritually, psychologically, sociologically, and even physiologically. These very children are oftentimes failing academically because most of their mental energy is spent trying to acclimate and socialize with others outside their home—amid their social anxiety. And unfortunately because of this, conventional societal "wisdom" often views many of these children as "having something wrong with them" and are often "labeled" and "diagnosed" with some type of "disorder" such as "ADD," "ADHD," "autism," "anxiety," "depression," and so on. Moreover, many of these children are often then prescribed various types of medications for their "diagnosis" which are nothing more than a toxic solution and a "quick fix" to a much bigger problem. A problem that perpetually falls through the cracks of a broken mental health system that is often reluctant to address the real issue at hand. Whereas, if the child were to have received the appropriate help and care, by perhaps removing them from the toxic and unhealthy environment in which they are being raised, outcomes could be or could have been very different. Now, let me be clear here, there are other factors that can cause and contribute to cognitive decline and psychological impediments within a child. Such as the common American diet, where most foods (including liquids) are either genetically modified or are poisoned with chemicals and/or other synthetic substances. Which is why even at birth, children are discovered to have impediments of various types because the mother had already been consuming the common American diet while the baby was in utero. If a person were to step back to see the forest through the trees and of what is truly going on in the lives of many children, they will see that most of these children do not need another "diagnosis" and/or "label." But what these children do need are parents who can provide them with a healthy, stable, loving, and functional environment in which they can thrive and survive. Even more, what these children need are parents who seek daily to honor the 5th commandment by having an intimate and loving relationship with not only their children, but with God Himself (the Ultimate Father and Mother). Moreover, society itself could also play its part by denormalizing children who are loud, aggressive, overbearing, selfish, and conceited; nevertheless, much of what continues to be further taught and enabled by society and by parents themselves. You see, a child does not have the same cognitive capability nor functional ability as that of an adult; therefore, they are not able to sort through emotional situations like the common adult can. Sadly, I have witnessed many grown adults who, in the presence of their own children, were degrading and even slandering other children because of their psychological and sociological impediments. And it is for this reason, along with many others, why many children grow up having no concept of what it means or what it even looks like to honor someone, because it was never taught or emulated by their parents; yet, they are to "Honor their father and mother?" So not only are children essentially being taught by their parents how to dishonor others, but this type of behavior pushes the child further and further away from developing any kind of relationship with God, even as they grow into adulthood. However, praise the Lord our God who is able to pull many of these children out of darkness and into His wonderful and glorious light, especially as they grow older and are away from their parents' dictatorship. It is clear that conventional societal "wisdom" has the propensity to label children, but this same "wisdom" has the proclivity to also apply labels to adults as well. With terms or labels such as psychopaths, sociopaths, narcissists, and so on. Oftentimes, it is said that these various psychological characteristics can overlap each other. Which, of course they do, why wouldn't they overlap? Because the characteristics are all derived from the same source—evil, the devil. Consider this: if a baby cries but then also coos, should we say that the baby has a crying disorder but then also has a cooing disorder? No, we call it as it is; the baby cries and the baby coos; it's a baby, and that's what babies do. Therefore, evil in all of its forms is simply just that—it's evil, nothing more and nothing less. But because society (predominantly Western society) doesn't want to face the truth and reality that the devil even exists, nor the fact that people themselves also have evil in their hearts, they will therefore diminish the devil down to a myth while applying various types of man-made "diagnoses" and/or labels to people who do evil. Which is precisely what the devil wants, by the way; because when humans apply terminology and labels unto each other, it essentially takes the heat, the spotlight, and burden off the devil himself. Furthermore, how often do you hear, or when was the last time you heard a family member call another family member evil? Rarely, but instead, they were likely given a label and were said to be narcissistic, or a liar, or a wretch, or maybe even a psychopath or a sociopath, just not evil. Which, again, in doing this, it only just further diminishes or even disregards the fact that the devil and evil exist. Therefore, leading people to quickly shift all blame onto each other and/or God and do so without further consideration of the fact that Satan has power over people and that people have evil in them. And is all the more reason why we all need Jesus in our hearts and in our lives; because Satan has no power or authority over Jesus Christ. Which, if God wanted, He could destroy Satan this very moment; however, God doesn't because it's not part of His current and much bigger plan. In the next passage you are about to read, Jesus spoke some very profound yet vociferous words during His ministry here on Earth. Words that should resonate and make a person ponder very deeply about the realities of life, but even more so, the type of relationships they may have with their earthly family:

Matthew 10:34-38

"Do not think that I have come to bring peace to the earth. I have not come to bring peace, but a sword. For I have come to set a man against his father, and a daughter against her mother, and a daughter-in-law against her mother-in-law. And a person's enemies will be those of his own household. Whoever loves father or mother more than me is not worthy of me, and whoever loves son or daughter more than me is not worthy of me. And whoever does not take his cross and follow me is not worthy of me. Whoever finds his life will lose it, and whoever loses his life for my sake will find it."

First, let me point out to you that Jesus (God) upon coming to Earth in flesh and speaking what He did in Matthew 10:34-38 was not a sudden change of mind on His part—as if the 5th commandment to "Honor your father and mother" was nullified. This passage only further corroborates that from the beginning, God's 5th commandment has always been about Him and not our earthly parents. Moreover, if you can fully conceptualize the reality and the occurrences of this passage, it's irrefutable that this holds to be true, even to this day. Yet, most households and the peoples within them deny this very fact and its occurrence as they disallow themselves from facing its truth. Moreover, if you find this passage and concept difficult to comprehend, then I encourage you to pray and to ponder deeply about the relationships that you have, and to seek counsel if necessary. Because if you are someone who continuously struggles with family relations, then you may be engaging and involving yourself within environments and relationships where you shouldn't be. Especially if the relationships are a detriment to your well-being. In Matthew 10:34-38, Jesus is not conveying that He is specifically and directly going to turn people against each other or that He is going to cause people to act out in evil ways. What Jesus is saying is that as He brings truth and convictions upon the people from within households, it will innately cause divisions because of how sin and evil are being exposed. Therefore, those within households will turn against each other as they act out sin and evil towards each other; however, for those who have chosen Christ over sin and evil, they will turn away from those who live in perpetual sin because they are toxic to that person's well-being. Jesus Himself does not turn people into enemies, nor does He turn people against each other—Jesus hates evil, it is people themselves who, as they do evil, will create and become enemies amongst themselves. Moreover, people become enemies when they are prideful, arrogant, selfish, and when they lie, cheat, steal, exploit, hate, envy, resent, gossip, and so on. Whereas, for those within households who are disciples of Jesus Christ, will in various ways see and experience the evil and sinful nature of their earthly family and how they live in sin without repentance or acknowledgment of it. Which in turn, just as Jesus stated, it will innately cause dichotomies within families and their households; because light and darkness cannot cohabitate within the same realm—not for extended periods of time anyways:

John 1:5

"And the light shineth in darkness; and the darkness comprehended it not."

Think of it this way: there is the "household" of evil and

then there is the "household" of God; these are two very different places and are divided and separated for very significant reasons. If we were to use the analogy of a household and assimilate it to the entire world of humanity but on a much larger scale of course, we see how the world is essentially a larger scale of a household; where the devil (evil and darkness) and Jesus (Light and Glory) cohabitate together here on Earth (for now). However, as we see, this is all occurring not without ongoing tension and opposition. Therefore, like that of a household, Jesus through division is separating the "wheat from the chaff" and will do so entirely come that final day of His return:

Matthew 3:12

"His winnowing fork is in his hand, and he will clear his threshing floor and gather his wheat into the barn, but the chaff he will burn with unquenchable fire."

Jesus at one point during His ministry here on Earth encountered two different men who wanted to follow Him, with each of the two men wanting to turn back and tend to family matters first before continuing on with Jesus. However, Jesus being very transparent yet concise, spoke these words:

Luke 9:59-60

"To another he (Jesus) said, 'Follow me.' But he (the man) said, 'Lord, let me first go and bury my father.' And Jesus said to him, 'Leave the dead to bury their own dead. But as for you, go and proclaim the kingdom of God.'"

In this passage, we see the reality (much like what we saw earlier in Matthew 10:34-38) of what it truly means to follow Jesus and that of what it means to live for the Kingdom of God. But even more, we see how this passage further parallels many others and how they nullify the premise that the 5th commandment has anything to do with our earthly parents—but has everything to do with God and honoring Him. One might ask, how is this so? Because God is not going to on one hand command everyone to "Honor their earthly father and mother," but then as He did with this man, turn around and tell him to completely disregard his father, mother, and family, as if they are all dead. Which is exactly what Jesus did; therefore, further confirming that the 5th commandment is all about God and not earthly parents. In this man's situation, if the 5th commandment was truly intended for earthly fathers and mothers, then Jesus would have said to the man that he should go bury his father while tending to his mother and family who were still alive (physically that is), but Jesus didn't. But instead, Jesus said to the man: "Let the dead bury the dead." By saying this, Jesus is alluding to the fact that the rest of this man's family or at least all who were with him, which likely could have been his mother, brothers, sisters, and so on, were all spiritually dead (though they were alive physically). Now, let me reiterate and further clarify some facts here before we get too far into this; God commands every one of us to love and honor all people. Thus, just because Jesus told this man to "Follow me" and to "Let the dead bury the dead" doesn't automatically mean that the man did not still love and honor his father and the rest of his family, as God commands us all to do. It's pointing to the fact that when Jesus says, "Come follow me," He means it. But not only does Jesus mean it, He is saying that when you hear His voice and calling, you have one opportunity (which is now in this lifetime) to drop everything, to give up living for anything or anyone and to give your life over to Him first and foremost. And if that means leaving behind those who are spiritually dead because they themselves disregarded the opportunity to also follow Jesus, then that's on them. Let me put it another way. What Jesus is saying to this man who wants to go back and bury his father is this: anyone who chooses to look back into the past to what is already done and to what can't be undone is not keeping their eyes fixed on Jesus and on that of what is eternal—which is the Kingdom of God and eternal life. Jesus is essentially telling this man to not only give up what is in the past but to give up his worldly view of "honoring" the dead, as it holds no value. Which is why Jesus expressly states, "Leave the dead to bury their own dead." What a person must come to understand is that when people pass from this earth and go to heaven, they will have no recollection of their past or time here on earth. Therefore, for those who have accepted Jesus Christ as Lord and Savior, upon entering God's Kingdom, will not know each other as they did here on earth; they will know each other, but not in the same way. Thus, in heaven a person will not know their children, their parents, their spouse, etc., as they knew them here on earth—which by the way, is not just my perspective, but is based on scripture and how it tells of this in many ways. Now, as for the man who wanted to turn back to bury his dead father; if you are familiar with scripture and if you recall what happened to Lot's wife, who, as they were running away from the corrupt and debaucherous city of Sodom—God turned Lot's wife into a pillar of salt because she turned to look back just after God had commanded them not to. Thus, God turned Lot's wife into a pillar of salt (literally) because she disobeyed God and turned to look back as fire and brimstone were raining down upon the city. Why did Lot's wife look back? She looked back because she was more focused and concerned for her past and present life and those she was in relation with than she was of her salvation and eternal future with God. Now, moving on, we've come to the second man who also wants to follow Jesus but first wants to interact with his family before doing so. In this passage, which parallels the last, Jesus answers this man in a similar fashion as the last:

Luke 9:61-62

"Yet another said, 'I will follow you, Lord, but let me first say farewell to those at my home.' Jesus said to him, 'No one who puts his hand to the plow and looks back is fit for the kingdom of God.'"

Here we see again, Jesus not only telling this man to leave his past behind but that this man is to also leave those of his household behind—his family and his friends. Once again, Jesus does not say to this man that he should dishonor his family and friends as if they don't exist. But what Jesus is saying is that He and the Kingdom of God are more important than family and friends and that He holds the keys to eternal life. Jesus is forthrightly telling this man to stop living merely for his family and friends and to stop making them out to be more than what they really are—as if they can save him from sin and eternal death. This man to whom Jesus was having this conversation with may have been a husband or may have been a young man who was nearing the age of adulthood and was about to leave his parents' household. Or maybe this man, like the last man from Luke 9:59-60, was living within a household of people who were spiritually dead because not one of them had any kind of relationship with Jesus Christ. Either way, in both scenarios, Jesus is telling these men to come follow Him and to give their lives over to Him. Yet, one might still be asking, why would Jesus tell someone, as it were for the two men in the passages of Luke, to leave their friends or family behind, isn't that unloving? The simple and quick answer is no, it's not unloving. Here's an analogy to help you better understand: Let's say you are hiking through a forest with your friends and/or family when you suddenly notice that the forest has caught fire. Worse off, you see that the fire is rapidly growing and is quickly encompassing you as strong winds fuel the fire. And as you look around, there appears to be no way out. The smoke is becoming so heavy that others in the group are panicking and are wanting to run—despite you expressly telling them not to panic and run. As you slowly move forward through the smoke, you begin to lose sight of the others. You notice just up ahead that there is another path. You also notice that this path splits off in two ways and that there is a sign next to each path. The sign has two arrows, each arrow pointing in opposing directions; with one arrow pointing to the north and the other pointing to the south. Either way, both directions of the two paths appear to be leading you directly into the fire with no way out. However, as you look more closely, you see writing next to the arrow pointing to the south, which reads: "This way is the way of your friends and family and is the way they have chosen; from this point on, if you choose to continue down this path, you will be taking life into your own hands. Thus, once you reach the actual fire, I can't guarantee that you will make it out alive." However, there is the second arrow that points to the north; it reads: "This is the way, the truth, and the life; and if you give up full control of your circumstances and your life right here and now, you will by taking this path be saved from the unquenchable fire and death and will exit the fire unharmed. However, if you are to choose this path, it requires much faith and endurance." By now, you begin to smell the hairs on your body start to burn due to the heat; it's time for you to act. So, you quickly give up any control of your life and have decided to walk by faith and not by sight; therefore, you take the path to the north even though it looks to be leading you directly into the fire. And as you continue in haste up the arduous path to the north, you eventually find yourself next to a river that is flowing well enough for you to jump in. So, you jump into the river, and it carries you safely through and beyond the burning forest; you have now been saved and have made it out alive. However, sadly and unfortunately, for your family, who has always lived a life full of pride and arrogance, having to always be in control over everything, elected to take the path to the south. And because they wanted to remain in "control," they perished by fire, for eternity. So, you see, despite your best efforts to encourage or implore, you cannot force your family or anyone else to take a specific path. It's up to them to make the final choice, but you can still encourage them and save yourself in the process. And why wouldn't you save yourself? What good is it if you are dead right along with the rest of them? What do you have to gain by going down the same path as they, when you know inevitably it leads to death? When, nevertheless, your only gain is death. Which, obviously, is no gain at all; it's only a loss; because once you are dead, you are dead. It's not like your family and friends while they are dead have any knowledge as to whether you are dead or whether you are alive; and if you are dead, it's not like you are aware of whether your family is dead or whether they are alive. Therefore, save yourself from spiritual death while you can, so that when you pass from this earth, you can live on for eternity in God's Kingdom. In this scenario, why did the family not want to give up their control over the fire situation, knowing that if they had, it would have likely saved their life? Was it because the fire had them so emotionally consumed that they couldn't make a decision? Likely not, but it would be a "good excuse" for them to use, and many do use it; but, either way, they still had a choice to make. Was it the smoke that blinded them from making the right choice? No, it was their pride, ego, and arrogance that made them blind to the truth and reality of what was truly happening right before their very own eyes. This very thing happens every day in real life as so many people are consumed by their own pride, ego, and arrogance that it blinds them from seeing and hearing the truth. They are blinded by the fleeting things of this world: riches, success, fame, validation, legacies. Which is why so many people willingly forfeit their soul to eternal death rather than give up control of their life here and now; because all they see and want is the now. The final summation is this: if you find yourself aboard a sinking ship with others, knowing that you all are about to perish, wouldn't you take the one and only life-saving offer given to you, even if it was by faith and even if it was being provided by someone else? Whereas, the only other alternative is death. Therefore, what do you have to lose? You just as well take the one and only option that lies before you, even if you don't fully understand it. Moreover, now that you yourself have been saved from a sinking ship, you now know what a sinking ship looks like; thus, you can now lead others to becoming saved by throwing them a life-vest—with this life vest being Jesus Christ. By now, I hope that you are seeing the way and hearing the truth of what it truly means to follow Jesus and how it requires you to take on an entirely new perspective of how you view life and the world around you. But even more so, how God the Father is truly the ultimate Father and Mother and how our earthly family should never get in the way of our decision to accept Jesus Christ as Lord and Savior. The apostle Paul in his letter to the church of Corinth talks about how there is natural division taking place within this world because Light (Jesus) and darkness (evil) have no common place for each other. How we as the church and as disciples of Jesus Christ are "temples" of the Light (the Holy Spirit) and that we who are in the Light are not to be unequally yoked with those who live in darkness:

2 Corinthians 6:14-16

"Do not be yoked together with unbelievers. For what do righteousness and wickedness have in common? Or what fellowship can light have with darkness? What harmony is there between Christ and Belial (the devil)? Or what does a believer have in common with an unbeliever? What agreement is there between the temple of God and idols? For we are the temple of the living God. As God has said: 'I will live with them and walk among them, and I will be their God, and they will be my people.'"

In His relationship with you, Jesus is not looking for partiality or division; He wants you entirely for Himself. And as we've been seeing from within the many passages of Scripture, not only is Jesus Christ Lord and Savior, but He also wants to be and can be your ultimate Father, Mother, Brother, Sister, and Friend. He wants to be your everything, and rightfully so—He created you and gave His life for you. Jesus is the only way to the Father; we cannot come to God through our parents nor anyone else for that matter, and neither does anyone else nor our parents get to dictate whether we come to Jesus or not. God chose us, and all we need to do in return is to choose Him. Even as helpless children we are ultimately and completely reliant on Jesus; without God not even our parents can provide for us—not without God Himself providing to our parents first. Which is all the more reason why God commands EVERYONE, more specifically those who are adult parents—to "Honor your Father and Mother" (God). For it was God the Father—who from the beginning—bore us in spirit; and who will again, take us in spirit from this earth. Let Wisdom and Truth lead the Way.

Psalm 139:16

"Your eyes saw my unformed substance; in your book were written, every one of them, the days that were formed for me, when as yet there was none of them."

Psalm 139:13-14

"For you formed my inward parts; you knitted me together in my mother's womb. I praise you, for I am fearfully and wonderfully made. Wonderful are your works; my soul knows it very well."

1 Corinthians 8:5-6

"For although there may be so-called gods in heaven or on earth—as indeed there are many "gods" and many "lords"—yet for us there is one God, the Father, from whom are all things and for whom we exist, and one Lord, Jesus Christ, through whom are all things and through whom we exist."

A CHILD IS A GIFT BESTOWED UPON US ALL

Psalm 127:3
"Behold, children are a heritage of the Lord, the fruit of the womb a reward."
Without God, there are no children; without children, there are no parents; without God, there are neither parents nor children. A child is a gift and blessing from the Lord; a child is not something that is to be treated as a possession but rather is a being that is to be cherished. A child is not to be looked upon as an object to which can be used as a means to fulfill the deep inner void that humanity has in our hearts—a deep void that only Jesus Christ can fulfill. A child is not something that is given from God for the purpose of a parent to control, manipulate, and mold into their own self-limiting perspectives, desires, and expectations but rather is a being that is to be led and guided with love. In the idea that the child's parents or guardians are to work alongside the Holy Spirit by instilling their most valuable attributes; such as love, joy,

peace, patience, kindness, goodness, faithfulness, gentleness, and self-control. And if the child is indeed raised in a God-like household, then in return, as the child grows and matures, they will reciprocate and bestow upon their parents and others these very same qualities and attributes. The objective as a parent is for them to provide the child with the necessary means to grow into an independent, responsible, authentic, genuine, compassionate, God-fearing adult who can eventually function on their own in society as an adult. In doing so, and through a parent's ongoing encouragement—as the child grows into adulthood, they will be more equipped and prepared as they encounter the trials and tribulations of life. However, many parents attempt to suppress, shield, and overprotect their children from the world and will do so by keeping the child contained and confined to the perimeters of a parent's preconceived and prefabricated realm of "safety." Parents, upon their inherent need to control, often claim to be "protecting" their child from the many harms and troubles of this world, but in reality, are hindering the child from overcoming and surpassing the fears and impediments that have long plagued the parents themselves. And by doing so, parents prevent their child from experiencing situations in life that would have otherwise provided the child with further growth and maturity; but even more, the parents hinder the child from developing a relationship with God through faith, where they would otherwise be learning to rely more on God and not themselves or their parents. It is not uncommon to hear a parent make the statement as such: "How they have (in many ways) "sacrificed" themselves and everything in life for the sake of their child." Essentially implying that the parents have fallen "victim" to their own premise of having a child while eliciting the "woe is me" mentality. The moment a parent adheres to the ideology that they are "sacrificing" themselves for their children, is when they have begun to believe that God and/or society owes them something for their "sacrificial services"—even though it was neither God or society that forced them into having children, though it has now and somehow turned into a "sacrificial" offering of themselves. If this isn't backdoor conceitedness, then I'm not sure what is. Are parents now "sacrificing" themselves on the cross so that their children may be saved from sin and death? This foolish line of thinking is likened to those who say, "God owes me something because I "sacrifice" myself by going to work every day, not only to earn a living but to contribute to society." Because of these common ideologies, oftentimes, children become the crutch of a parent's relationship; as the child becomes the footstool of the parent's ongoing dissensions and discontentments. And amid the parents' ongoing resentment and bitterness, they passively and emotionally abuse the child with shame and guilt for the duration of the child's life, even into adulthood. You see, we all have free will to make our own decisions and choices in life, choices to even have children. Had God not given us free will, we, for all intents and purposes, would be robots; and robots can't love, and neither can they have relationships. And because of our sinful nature and free will, we have a world that has gotten itself into a perpetual predicament. A predicament where people are having children for all the wrong reasons; reasons that have taken on a whole new meaning. Children are now being viewed as objects for which they have become subjects to the many selfish desires of mankind. In the earliest days, this came to fruition when children became objects of labor; meaning, the more children a family had, the more work that could be accomplished in a shorter period, which also meant more revenue. And although these same occurrences continue to happen, much of what we see today are children who have become the "quick fix" to loneliness and failing marriages. But it doesn't just stop there. We see children being born simply for the purpose of parents having to pay less in taxes, or to obtain a leave of absence from the "daily grind" or work-life because the parent is tired of the rut that they have found themselves in. Moreover, upon becoming pregnant, the parent now gets to take advantage of maternity leave; and for many, come the hopes of never having to return to work again. Sadly, I've been a witness to many ongoing adult-sibling rivalries where the premise of having children had merely become a competition. Rivalries such as wanting to be the first to have a child, or to be the one to have the most children. I have had many conversations with adults who, from their siblings, family members, or even by their friends, have been shamed because they elected not to have children. I, myself, though I love children and have spent much of my life around them and caring for them, have also been shamed by others for not having children of my own. In one specific instance—because I had a change of mind from what I previously said about wanting to have children—was shamed because the parent wanted me to feel their resentment as they elected to have children and were now in some manner regretting it. And though this parent loved their children, they resented the fact that I wasn't experiencing the difficulties of parenthood, as they were. It has been said to me more times than I would ever like to have heard; parents who have expressly said to me that they wished they would have never had children. And in their own subtle way through their own choice words, discreetly alluded to the fact that they even have regret in doing so. Moreover, many of them would then go on further in advising me not to have children. Many of you, like myself, have heard at least one parent (or many), say to someone who is not a parent: "You have to be a parent to understand" or "You wouldn't know because you don't have kids." Oftentimes, in hearing parents make these statements, you can hear and almost feel the regret, the resentment, the disdain, and even the despair in their voice as they speak these words. Aside from the fact that the words themselves are nothing more than a scapegoat for the parent's guilt in how they are struggling as a parent. Furthermore, upon a parent making these statements, what must be considered is that we all were kids at one point; and kids, even at a young age: come to see, to learn, and to know more than what a parent often wants to admit. Moreover, I know of many people who don't have children, yet they have a better understanding and connection to children than many couples who do have children. A person does not have to physically birth a child in order to develop, obtain, or feel the supernatural or spiritual bond that can occur between a child and another human being. For example: Look at the many parents who have adopted a child; yet their bond with that child is just as great as if they had birthed the child themselves. Therefore, a person does not have to be a parent themselves in order for them to understand the nuances of raising a child or what it entails to have a child in their care. Even as adults, whether a person is a parent or not, we are often "parenting" others; whether it be other adults or whether it be other people's children. And even for some of you, when you were a child and even now as an adult, have been "parenting your parents" for as long as you can remember (you know who you are, and you fully understand what I mean). So you see, despite anyone's age, we are all in some manner "parenting" each other, and God has structured it to be this way. This is one of many reasons as to why God tells us—even as adults—to remain humble at all times and to "not think of yourself as being more highly than you ought to" (Romans 12:3). It is the very reason why God has given each of us our very own unique gifts and talents, so that we can help, lead, guide, instruct, teach, and ultimately serve each other. If this weren't true, then it wouldn't be so prevalent in the fact that many adults often turn to an outside source—such as another adult, mentor, or counselor—in order to address issues within their own lives, marriages, or families? Many mentors or counselors are not married, and neither do they have children, yet they counsel and mentor others who are married and have children. Even people with the highest degrees of education such as psychiatrists, psychologists, sociologists, therapists, etc., are not impervious or exempt from the brokenness of humanity; they all have their own issues as well, just like the rest of humanity. There is not a single person here on this earth that does not in some manner contend with some type of personal issues or brokenness. Which is why we see God using whomever He pleases and how He pleases as a vessel to minister to others. God does not need someone to have a Phd in order for Him to use that person as a vessel to minister and help someone else. As I write this, child and adult suicide is at an all-time high, with divorce rates higher than ever before; and none of this is merely coincidental. As we know, children are sponges; they see, hear, speak, and emulate anything and almost all things of a parent. Empirical evidence has shown that a child's brain is often not fully developed until they reach their early to mid-20s and in some cases not until around the age of 30. Thus, most children in their early years of life do not have the cognitive ability to understand nor to truly conceptualize or to fully rationalize right from wrong, not like that of an adult. Therefore, if a child is raised in an environment where people are to love and honor one another and other people, then it is often likely what they will do. However, if a child is raised in an environment where they are shown to condemn and to hate, that is likely what they will do. We know that whatever environment a child is raised in, that environment is who and what the child predominantly becomes. Now, of course, one could argue that this is not some hard and fast rule and that this can be relative, especially for the child that was not raised in the common household but was raised on the street by some form of society. However, it is not uncommon for parents to use relativism as an excuse to pardon themselves from their own child's nefarious behavior; as they neglect to take responsibility, seeking to place blame on everyone and everything, but themselves. Which is why it is imperative for a parent to come to terms with the truth and reality that their daily actions and choices can literally make or break a child for life. For example, I have witnessed many parents who will get drunk on alcohol and will do so while their children are often present, but then in pure ignorance and hypocrisy, they will punish their children severely when they get into trouble and are caught with alcohol. The concept of this alcohol scenario can be applied to just about any other parent-child situation, where a child gets into trouble for the very thing their parents had taught and shown them. I once knew of a man who was very manipulative towards others and would often intentionally "push other people's buttons" purely for entertainment, as if it was a game to him. Eventually, this man became a parent, and as I watched him interact with his child, I witnessed him on several occasions teaching his child how to emotionally manipulate others; not only through words but even through actions. In seeing this, I had come to realize more deeply the meaning behind Luke 17:1-2, how it describes what is to come for those who do not cease from their wicked ways and cause children to sin in the process:

Luke 17:1-2

"And he said to his disciples, 'Temptations to sin are sure to come, but woe to the one through whom they come! It would be better for him if a millstone were hung around his neck and he were cast into the sea than that he should cause one of these little ones to sin.'"

Oftentimes, within the thought of having children, couples will endeavor to conjure up any possible reason—especially if it works in their favor—to move forward with having a child. Thus, amid their emotions running high, they quickly forget the realities of life and of what is truly required of them in becoming a parent. Disregarding any rational aspects as to why it might be best for them to not have children, especially if their objective is to have something "new and exciting" in their life. A very common objective that many can relate to is the idea of owning a house or a car (oftentimes, one either of which a person often cannot afford or does not need). And because we live in the USA where the idea of living within our means is so primitive, most will indulge. Therefore, most people end up buying more than what they bargained for; thus, within a short period and as their emotions wind down, they find themselves contending with regret and buyer's remorse. Moreover, they now want to return the expensive oversized house or car because they did not logically think through the purchase; but instead, they allowed their feelings and emotions to dictate their decisions. Though a person cannot sell or return a child like a person can with many other things; sadly, many people have tried. Having a child is a lifelong commitment, and in the first 18 years of a child's life (or at least until the child moves out of the house to live on their own), a parent's life should encompass that child. However, let me be clear here, I don't mean in an unhealthy literal sense; such as the parent or parents whose lives revolve around their children in a sense of idolization as if the child is their sole purpose and reason for living. What I am saying here is that when a parent elects to have a child, it is their full responsibility to raise that child in a loving, caring, unselfish, God-like manner with the ultimate goal being that the child will one day need to function in life on their own as an adult. With also keeping in mind that the child may one day become a parent themselves, so that they can raise their children up in a God-like manner with the intent of them also having an intimate relationship with God. Upon becoming a parent, a parent must come to terms with the fact that once a child becomes an adult and as they go out into the world on their own, their parents will not be around forever. Thus, the parents should teach their child to not assume that they will always have their parents to "fall back on" for when life doesn't go according to plan. Especially when it comes to money and resources. There is already an overwhelming number of parents that attempt in many ways to "buy" their way into the hearts of their children through their money and resources. Which only just furthers the already enabled entitlement mindset; as the child eagerly awaits and looks forward to the future of receiving their parents' inheritance once their parents pass away. And because of this common occurrence, many children even before their parents pass away, don't even think twice about indulging in life's materialism because they put stock in eventually receiving the inheritance they assume is coming to them. When it comes to parents having children and of what is commonly seen today, are couples who go on having children but do so as if the children are essentially nonexistent. Parents will disseminate their children amongst various people as if they are an object, an object that is getting in the way of the parents' own selfish ambitions of chasing after money, "success," and "security." Parents will pass their child around from daycare to school, or to a friend's house, then to sports, then to grandparents, and then back home just for them to essentially eat, sleep, play with their phone or a video game, to then begin the cycle again the next day. Therefore, what we have are many children who are being raised by just about everyone else, other than by the parents themselves. Which is no wonder why chaos and disorder ensue within so many households because the children have no foundation from which they can base anything on. Moreover, because a child has an undeveloped brain, the child does not have the cognitive ability to fully process or to work through all the varying degrees of expectations, personalities, and characteristics in which the child interacts throughout the day. Yet, many parents often wonder why they have such a difficult time connecting with their child and why their children don't respect them nor want to listen to them. Whereas, for the child that is not tossed around from one place or person to the next, will have a more structured life of consistency and repetition which naturally reinforces good behavior, provided that is what is shown to them. But even more, the child needs to be brought up in the teachings of what it is to have a healthy God-fearing and God-loving relationship with our Lord and Savior Jesus Christ; teachings of love, affection, compassion, and intimacy, and so on:

Deuteronomy 6:6-7

"And these words that I command you today shall be on your heart. You shall teach them diligently to your children and shall talk of them when you sit in your house, and when you walk by the way, and when you lie down, and when you rise."

However, if this is not occurring because parents are instead choosing to live for themselves as they pour out much of their energy and soul into their careers and/or social life rather than into the lives of their children, then the implications derived from this type of parent-child relationship will be devastating. Which is why it is not uncommon for there to be contentions that never seem to end between parents and children because the only relationship they have with each other is superficial and distant. Even from infancy, a superficial or distant relationship with a child drastically affects the parent-child relationship. Beginning from birth, there is an intrinsic supernatural connection that is to be maintained between the mother, the father, and the child; this connection should occur daily if you want the best outcome for the child—psychologically, sociologically, physiologically, and spiritually. So often, before a child is ever born, par-

ents will already have a mental list of preconceived notions of what they want and expect the child to be. Which often begins in the belief that the child will be the "one necessary thing" that will bring love, joy, peace, happiness, and contentment into their relationship and marriage. However, this line of thinking is only just the beginning of many disappointments and let-downs because it does not align with reality. How so, you ask, because this line of thinking is out of order—the placement of ideals is disordered—because it is NOT the child's duty to bring love, joy, peace, happiness, and contentment into the life of a parent or into their marriage or relationship. And how dare parents place such a burden on an unborn child. If you don't perceive this concept to be real, then explain why it is that hundreds to thousands of babies every year are shaken to death by their parents because of frustration and anger. So you see, it is first and foremost the parent's duty, obligation, and responsibility (not the child's) to bring love, joy, peace, and happiness into the life of their child. When this occurs within its correct order, there is a paradoxical effect that supernaturally takes place between the child and the parent; the child will intrinsically return to its parents the love, peace, joy, and happiness that was first shown to them. But then as the child begins to grow and mature, is when things become complicated. Because this is when the child really begins to disrupt the parents' preconceived notions for the child's life and theirs. Which oftentimes brings forth manipulations, coercions, exercised "power" and "authority" in an attempt to "fear" the child into submission as the parents endeavor to conform and mold the child to their expectations versus God's expectations:
Ephesians 6:4

"Fathers do not provoke your children to anger but bring them up in the discipline and instruction of the Lord." Oftentimes, many parents will wittingly—though for some unwittingly—find themselves living within their own lifelong regrets because they did not meet their own personal objectives and expectations that they had set for themselves early on in their own lives. Therefore, they will attempt to impose their own unmet goals, aspirations, and expectations onto their children in the idea that their children will be the ones to indemnify their lifelong regrets. Thus, in doing so, parents delude themselves in the idea that they are able to accomplish their unfulfilled objectives through the lives of their children, in the belief that their lifelong self-regret will eventually dissipate. However, this of course never works, never mind the fact that this concept is utterly selfish in the parents' attempt to do so. And because of this, the child suffers greatly for it throughout life and oftentimes even into adulthood as the child struggles and battles with ongoing feelings of incompetency and inadequacy. But then there is another side to this ideological parenting spectrum: where we see parents who have met their own long-sought-after goals and expectations in life; as they have in many ways become "successful" (that is, successful according to their own personal standards and definitions). Therefore, as it goes, these same parents will come to expect the same kind of "success" from their own children as well. Thus, through "power" and "authority," the parents will scheme, manipulate, guilt, and shame, in their attempt to control and conform their child or adult-child into reaching the same level of "success." Which again, does nothing more but to cause extensive damage to the heart, soul, and mind of that child. And as we

know, many of these children, even into adulthood, have the proclivity to become "people-pleasers"; versus someone who can love themselves and others without feeling the need to compensate through the premise of people-pleasing. But, because the child is often attempting to live up to everyone else's expectations and standards, they fail to thrive because they never see themselves as being good enough:

Colossians 3:21

"Fathers do not provoke your children, lest they become discouraged."

The premise of children becoming objects to meet the objectives of their parents does not just simply cease at the parental realm; sadly, it goes much further than that. Derived from the psychology realm, many have heard the term "The devouring mother" or maybe even "The devouring parents." However, has it ever occurred, as it has to me, that one could liken this idiom—along with its very same characteristics—to describe what I relate to as "The devouring grandparents." Because, much like "The devouring mother," "The devouring grandparents" spend much of their time with the grandkids in an attempt to compensate for the lack of fulfillment they have within. For "The devouring grandparents," oftentimes much of their time spent with their grandchildren comes with an attempt to indemnify or compensate for their own failed parenting, which occurred within the relationship of their own children. And so now, the grandparents endeavor endlessly to vindicate themselves by smothering their grandchildren with "love," affection, and attention, and will do so in any possible way for their own self-gratification. Which also and often includes smothering the grandchildren with their money and resources as they attempt to "buy" their way into the hearts of their grandchildren. And much like "The devouring mother (or father)," "The devouring grandparents" will "love" their grandkids for selfish reasons and not for selfless reasons. Much like "The devouring mother," the grandparents will do whatever it takes to earn the attention, affection, and love of the children, even if it means giving up their own dignity. Thus, like "The devouring mother," "The devouring grandparents" seek to have a close "bonding" relationship with their grandkids in an attempt to fill the deep empty void they have within themselves; the deep empty void that only Jesus Christ can fulfill. Like "The devouring mother," the grandparents will strive endlessly to be the center of their grandkids 'needs and attention and will justify their actions all "for the sake of love." When in all reality, deep down, they are doing it first and foremost for their own selfish reasons for which they will never admit. Now, this isn't to say that the grandparents don't love their grandchildren; most often they do. However, like "The devouring mother," their agendas and prerogatives precede and supersede what would otherwise be selfless love. Thus, what we often see are grandparents who will completely overlook any personal boundaries of their own, and all other boundaries for that matter, as they strive to meet the child's wants and needs because once again, they are doing it all "for the sake of love." For example: the grandparents will often purchase things or will allow the grandchildren to do things or to have things that the child's parents would otherwise never allow. And by doing so, they are teaching their grandchildren that rules and obediences are only just relative and that rules and obediences are merely contingent upon who they are with. Which also further reinforces and enables the "entitlement" mentality along with bad behavior. But even more, grandparents will indulge themselves in an ongoing game of "good parent" versus "bad parent"; where the grandparents strive in competition against each other—or even in competition against the parents—for the child's love and attention. Now, unless you have been living in a cave most of your life, you likely have heard almost every grandparent say something like this: "Because we are the grandparents, we are "entitled" to "spoil" our grandchildren." This proclamation by the grandparents is not only arrogant, ignorant, and selfish, but it further enables the implemented "entitlement" ideology that conventional society already and perpetually reinforces. Moreover, it completely disregards all personal boundaries that have already been implemented between the child and its parents—as the grandparents come along with their "entitlement" propaganda endeavoring to nullify and override any of these boundaries. But then the irony is this: upon the grandparents making void and overriding boundaries that were initially implemented by the children's parents, the grandparents will pontificate on how "This generation of children has no respect for their parents and does not listen to their elders," and how "This generation feels so entitled." So not only do the grandparents for their own propaganda want to be the center of attention, but will often attempt to demonstrate "control" over the children and their parents. The entire concept of these common occurrences is egregious, yet it happens every day amongst parents, grandparents, and grandchildren, and so many parents allow it to happen. So why does it happen? Let me explain: it happens because parents themselves do not have personal boundaries. It happens because parents themselves oftentimes have their own propaganda and motives that they are endeavoring to live out. Because you see, if the parents disrupt the agendas and motives of the grandparents, then the grandparents disrupt the agendas and motives of the parents; it's a perpetual mind-game of manipulation between them all. Furthermore, if the parents upset the grandparents by not allowing them to do-as-they-please, this could lead to possibly having no grandparents as a backup plan for additional financial resources and other securities for if it were needed (and is the real reason why parents upon having children will often move back home where they are close to family). But then also, if the parents upset the grandparents, this could possibly mean giving up the convenience of having grandparents to watch the kids or to take the kids for however often is needed and at a moment's notice. Which in turn would equate to less time that the parents would have to themselves and for themselves. So, you see, it's often all about motives and agendas for both the parents and grandparents. And as the parents continue to allow the grandparents to do as they please with the grandkids, not only are they showing and teaching the kids that boundaries and rules are essentially negotiable and relative, but that it is possible to manipulate others in order to get what they want. And because children do not have the cognitive awareness to understand the circumstances in which they are being placed, this can be quite confusing to them as they try to make sense of what is right from wrong. Especially when the children are being corrected by their parents regarding a set of rules, but then are not being corrected by the grandparents regarding the same set of rules of which were implemented by the parents. So, not only are the grandparents creating an environment that is confusing and unhealthy for the child, but they are also completely disrespecting the parents in the process as the parents attempt to set rules and boundaries for their child. Moreover, not only are the grandparents destroying the boundaries that have been implemented by the parents themselves, but they are damaging the relationship between the child and the parents because of it. Remember, a child has no choice nor say in any of this; the child is at the complete mercy of their parents' and grandparents' choices and actions. Children, all too often, are used as a scapegoat for the many choices and situations that parents have otherwise put themselves in. Therefore, parents will use their children as an excuse to cover up and conceal a parent's or parents' long-lived bad habits and flaws that they otherwise have not dealt with but have been ignoring most of their life. That said, I want to draw your attention to one final concept that has proven to cause so much devastation to a child's well-being as they become a witness to the destruction of two beings. There is a common idiom and ideology which many of us have heard and is all too often said by many parents who have been considering divorce or separation of some manner. The idiom often goes something like this: "We're staying together for the kid's sake." Undoubtedly, every child has witnessed their parents arguing in some manner, but for many children, they have also been witnesses to their parents' destructive behavior towards each other as they verbally and physically abuse each other through complete emotional immaturity and selfishness. For a child, this type of environment leads to everlasting implications as it devours the child's heart, soul, mind, and strength. With ramifications that leave a child with long-term effects such as fear, anxiety, anger, insecurity, uncertainty, confusion, depression, lack of trust, and so on. Unfortunately, and all too often, the child will feel as if they were the root cause of the parents' ongoing contempt and resentment towards each other. Even more, as the parents become so hateful and resentful toward each other and as they take it upon themselves through whatever means possible to destroy one another, the child sits and watches terrified as they wonder what they had done wrong to upset their parents. Moreover, as the parents' communication and actions toward each other become hostile, the hostility overflows into the child, whether it be directly or indirectly. So not only does the child believe that they are the cause of their parents' behavior towards each other, they begin to believe that the rest of humanity functions in the same way. This is when the child will begin to create their own armor of defense as they construct many inner walls of protection within their heart. Which sadly, only ever promotes and further enables problematic habits and characteristics within the life of that child as they grow older; while their heart hardens and as love no longer leads the way. As parents continue to "stay together for the sake of the kids," but for selfish reasons and not for selfless reasons, they will endeavor to use each other for security purposes—predominantly for financial security. The fact of the matter is, they are simply using each other for the purposes of "getting by" without having to make any drastic changes or decisions. And even though their current situation is drastic and dramatic already—as they actively damage their relationship and their children—they are more concerned about their reputation as seen by others. Thus, the parents will continue living as they are, just without having the external show that would otherwise depict to others that anything is wrong. This is a prime example of how pride, arrogance, ego, stubbornness, and selfishness can lead to devastation and destruction. For many married couples, they cannot even fathom the premise of being single and alone; therefore, their actions are further fueled by selfishness as they "stay together for the sake of the kids." And as it were, even before the parents had become married with children, one or both parents were already contending with personal insecurities and the thought of being alone and single. Whereas, if Jesus Christ had been their ultimate love, purpose, and foundation in life, they would have less of an issue with being single and alone; and if they were to have decided to partake in marriage, it would have been for the right reasons and not selfish reasons. So, as the parents continue to live within a state of cohabitation and selfishness, the entire family structure continues to break down as the parents demonstrate to their children everything but love, mercy, grace, compassion, and humility. Thus, parents must consider their situation very wisely before they further indulge in conventional "wisdom," which says to "Stay together for the sake of the kids." But instead, ask themselves, who is this best for again, the kids or the parents?! I think it's safe to say that if parents were more apt to do what was truly best for their children versus what is more convenient and self-serving, it may have saved their children from having a front-row seat to watching two people attempt to destroy each other through ongoing hate, resentment, bitterness, infidelity, retaliation, addictions, and in many cases, the death of a parent or a child due to suicide. Now, let me clear here, I'm not condoning divorce, and neither does God, but if parents are relentlessly destroying each other because their pride is bigger than their love and humility, then I believe it's safe to say that divorce may be a better alternative. Especially when it's clear that the parents are not going to relent or seek help and are destroying the kids right along with themselves. Might this be one of several reasons as to why God through Moses permitted divorce:

Matthew 19:8

"Jesus replied, "Moses permitted divorce only as a concession to your hard hearts, but it was not what God had originally intended."

And perhaps once the parents distance themselves from each other and begin to think and see more clearly, they can turn from their selfishness and get their children the help they need so that they can begin to heal from the damage that has already been done. Many ongoing statistics along with empirical evidence itself have shown that children who come from a household of divorced parents are more prevalent to become divorced themselves. And while this may hold to be true, this is not to say that children who come from non-divorced households are any less problematic or dysfunctional than those coming from divorced households, and empirical evidence clearly proves this as well. Because if we were to look at the broader spectrum without biases and delusions, considering all factors and outcomes, I believe the evidence is clear to show that there is little to no partiality between the two circumstances. It is irrefutable that there are just as many couples, though they are not divorced, who merely cohabitate as their relationship is based on consumerism and not unconditional love. One could even make the case in saying that there is no delineation amongst the number of children who have committed heinous and evil acts and whether they came from a non-divorced household or a divorced household. Because it's not divorce that makes or breaks a child, it is the parents themselves who make or break a child. Parents who are non-divorced are no less selfish and have no less evil in their hearts than those who are divorced. This is not to say that it is always both parents who are conspiring against each other; oftentimes it can be just the one parent causing the most havoc. So you see, in either situation, there is only one solution: Jesus Christ. Whether divorced or non-divorced, parents need Jesus to come into their hearts in order to be transformed; a transformation that turns evil and selfishness into love, humility, and selflessness. Look at the many stories from within the Bible, beginning with Adam and Eve; they were not divorced, and look what occurred between their first two sons—one murdered the other. Throughout scripture, we see how Jesus often took the most broken people and transformed them into the most beautiful and devout Christians. As adults, the most important and powerful thing we can do for all children is to love them, pray for them, and lead them to the Lord. That as they grow into adulthood, they can obtain the wisdom and knowledge that comes through having a relationship with God; that they can recognize when they need help and will have the courage to ask for it. And for the children who come from broken parental households, we must pray that they find a good support system, receive counseling from others, all in the hopes that they don't fall into a life or marriage of what had been shown to them. And above all else, that these children can be led into living a healthier and more joyful life through having a strong and faithful relationship with Jesus Christ: He who can truly heal and mend a child's broken and abused heart. So, whether God has stewarded you with children of your own or whether you care for children that are not your own; children are a gift and a blessing from God and are not something we possess or own. God possesses them all; they are His, just as you are His. Therefore, honor children by honoring God—the ultimate Father and Mother of us all:

Matthew 19:14

"Jesus said, 'Let the little children come to me, and do not hinder them, for the kingdom of heaven belongs to such as these.'"

Romans 11:36

"For everything comes from Him and exists by His power and is intended for His glory. All glory to Him forever! Amen."

THE FATHER WEPT AND HE WEEPS FOR YOU—SO PUT YOUR TRUST IN HIM & BELIEVE

Matthew 10:28-33
"And do not fear those who kill the body but cannot kill the soul. Rather fear him who can destroy both soul and body in hell. Are not two sparrows sold for a penny? And not one of them will fall to the ground apart from your Father. But even the hairs of your head are all numbered. Fear not, therefore; you are of more value than many sparrows. So, everyone who acknowledges me before men, I also will acknowledge before my Father who is in heaven, but whoever denies me before men, I also will deny before my Father who is in heaven."
Honor and fear the Lord your Maker; for it is only He who can destroy flesh and soul. No one can take your life from you, not Satan or anyone else, not even your parents who in flesh bore you into this world. Even the abortion of an unborn fetus can't have its life taken, not without God first allowing it; even then, though its heart may stop, and its body may cease to function, the spirit of the fetus is still with God and in His care. You see, for all of us, it is in our nature, it is in our hearts and souls for us to want to worship, to praise, and to idolize something; this something was meant to be God Himself and He intended it to be this way from the beginning. Thus, if you have not given your worship, your praise, your heart and life over to Jesus Christ, then innately you have given it over to someone or something else. If you love someone more than God, then you have essentially made that person

your idol and your god. Whatever a person looks to as their identity, whether it be another person, money, success, career, etc., they will become enslaved to that thing because it is what controls their heart, soul, mind, and strength—it is what they live for. We see idolization happening within all kinds of relationships; whether it be a spouse who lives out every breath for the other, or whether it be a parent who in every aspect lives and breathes for their children. Most of us know of at least one person who lives their life just to please others, and does so for all the wrong reasons; therefore, that person has many gods, because they care more about what people think than that of what God thinks. We see all too often how people will even idolize themselves—as if they are god—as if they have created themselves and are sustaining themselves. Therefore, it is not uncommon for these same people to want to be in complete control of not only themselves, but of everyone and everything. Because their pride, their ego, and their arrogance have perpetually blinded them from seeing the truth and reality of who they are and of what they are doing. This is one of many reasons why our Lord Jesus Christ weeps for those who choose to follow their own ways, their own hearts, and the ways of this world, in lieu of following Him. What is quite profound and shouldn't be missed is how throughout Scripture we see how God will go so far as to allow the death of someone for the mere purpose of influencing and drawing others near to Him. In the passage you are about to read, you will see how Jesus allows His beloved friend Lazarus to be taken by death, due to an illness. Jesus uses the overall experience as a means to "awaken" others from being spiritually dead. Jesus not only allows the death of His beloved friend Lazarus to come to fruition but even delays His coming to him; and does so just to get His point across and to be heard. Furthermore, Jesus shows how the death of one's body is of no concern to Him and that death itself has no hold on anyone unless Jesus says so; even if it has been several hours or several days, it does not matter to Him. Jesus at one point even becomes indignant towards His friends as they mourn because His friends are not listening and believing in Him and in what He is telling them—that "This illness does not lead to death" and that He is the Son of God and that His powers are limitless. But then Jesus at the same time also becomes sorrowful and grievous, not because of the death of Lazarus but because He also feels the pain, hurt, and sorrow of what His friends are feeling. Jesus is depicting all the common emotions and feelings of a human, which show that He understands and empathizes with them. And not only was it for His beloved friends that Jesus was weeping; He was also weeping out of love, grief, sorrow, and empathy that He has for His friend Lazarus, knowing the pain and suffering that His beloved friend Lazarus endured prior to and upon his physical death. You see, just because Jesus foreknew that He was going to raise Lazarus back to life does not discount or diminish the fact that Lazarus suffered in pain and agony before his death. Preface: As you are about to read in the coming passage, one thing to keep in mind is that whenever there is mention in the Bible of someone falling or being "asleep" (as Jesus said about Lazarus), it just simply means that this person's physical body has no life or is dead. However, because they are a disciple of God, their spirit lives on with God:

John 11:1-44

"Now a certain man was ill, Lazarus of Bethany, the village of

Mary and her sister Martha. Mary was the one who anointed the Lord with perfume and wiped his feet with her hair; her brother Lazarus was ill. So the sisters sent a message to Jesus, 'Lord, he whom you love is ill.' But when Jesus heard it, he said, 'This illness does not lead to death; rather it is for God's glory, so that the Son of God may be glorified through it.' Accordingly, though Jesus loved Martha and her sister and Lazarus, after having heard that Lazarus was ill, he stayed two days longer in the place where he was. Then after this he said to the disciples, 'Let us go to Judea again.' The disciples said to him, 'Rabbi, the Jews were just now trying to stone you, and are you going there again?' Jesus answered, 'Are there not twelve hours of daylight? Those who walk during the day do not stumble, because they see the light of this world. But those who walk at night stumble, because the light is not in them.' After saying this, he told them, 'Our friend Lazarus has fallen asleep, but I am going there to awaken him.' The disciples said to him, 'Lord, if he has fallen asleep, he will be all right.' Jesus, however, had been speaking about his death, but they thought that he was referring merely to sleep. Then Jesus told them plainly, 'Lazarus is dead. For your sake I am glad I was not there, so that you may believe. But let us go to him.' Thomas, who was called the Twin, said to his fellow disciples, 'Let us also go, that we may die with him.' When Jesus arrived, he found that Lazarus had already been in the tomb for four days. Now Bethany was near Jerusalem, some two miles away, and many of the Jews had come to Martha and Mary to console them about their brother. When Martha heard that Jesus was coming, she went and met him, while Mary stayed at home. Martha said to Jesus, 'Lord, if you had been here, my brother would not have died. But even now I know that God will give you whatever you ask of him.' Jesus said to her, 'Your brother will rise again.' Martha said to him,

'I know that he will rise again in the resurrection on the last day.' Jesus said to her, 'I am the resurrection and the life. Those who believe in me, even though they die, will live, and everyone who lives and believes in me will never die. Do you believe this?' She said to him, 'Yes, Lord, I believe that you are the Messiah, the Son of God, the One coming into the world.' When she had said this, she went back and called her sister Mary, and told her privately, 'The Teacher is here and is calling for you.' And when she heard it, she got up quickly and went to him. Now Jesus had not yet come to the village, but was still at the place where Martha had met him. The Jews who were with her in the house, consoling her, saw Mary get up quickly and go out. They followed her because they thought that she was going to the tomb to weep there. When Mary came where Jesus was and saw him, she knelt at his feet and said to him, 'Lord, if you had been here, my brother would not have died.' When Jesus saw her weeping, and the Jews who came with her also weeping, he was greatly disturbed in spirit and deeply moved. He said, 'Where have you laid him?' They said to him, 'Lord, come and see.' Jesus began to weep. So the Jews said, "See how he loved him!" But some of them said, 'Could not he who opened the eyes of the blind man have kept this man from dying?' Then Jesus, again greatly disturbed, came to the tomb. It was a cave, and a stone was lying against it. Jesus said, 'Take away the stone.' Martha, the sister of the dead man, said to him," Lord, already there is a stench because he has been dead four days." Jesus said to her, 'Did I not tell you that if you believed, you would see the glory of God?' So they took away the stone. And Jesus looked upward and said, 'Father, I thank you for having heard me. I knew that you always hear me, but I have said this for the sake of the crowd standing here, so that they may believe that you sent me.' When he had said this, he cried with

a loud voice, 'Lazarus, come out!' The dead man came out, his hands and feet bound with strips of cloth, and his face wrapped in a cloth. Jesus said to them, 'Unbind him, and let him go.'"

So, you see, Jesus allowed Lazarus to die physically but not in spirit. Therefore, the death of Lazarus' physical body had essentially become a sacrifice for many with the intent to bring many to believe in Jesus Christ as Lord. It is obvious that God had this planned out well before it had ever taken place, which further shows that God is in control of all circumstances at all times. But even more, does not this narrative sound familiar to you, because it should—Jesus also sacrificed Himself to death for the entire world so that the entire world might be saved through Him, and that God would also be glorified in it. Thus, as you just read, not even physical death within this world can separate us from the love and relation of our heavenly Father. And though the death of our physical body is likely to come for us all, it is in essence, of no concern to God Himself. Furthermore, for us all: God preemptively knows what our precise date and time of our birth into this world was to be, just as He preemptively knows what our precise day and time of death will be when we leave this world. Continuing on from within the Bible, there is another narrative derived from the book of Exodus, where God, for various reasons, used the nefarious king of Egypt (Pharaoh) to carry out His will. But also to demonstrate His power and glory by showing that His power reigns over everything and everyone, including Pharaoh himself—who perceived himself to also be a god. However, God ended the life of Pharaoh by drowning him and his army in the Red Sea just after God had parted the sea so that the Israelites could escape and pass through it on dry ground. God, throughout this narrative, intentionally and perpetually allowed Pharaoh's heart to become "strengthened" (hardened) with evil, while God was further emphasizing and demonstrating His power over Pharaoh. Moreover, despite God providing Pharaoh with 10 opportunities through 10 plagues to repent—with the 10th plague even taking the life of Pharaoh's son—Pharaoh still neglected to repent. Within this narrative, we see again how God used the life and death of one man (Pharaoh) to show that He is the only true God who holds all power and glory and that there is no other. Now, one without knowledge and understanding might say, "Well, it seems quite selfish of God to allow a person to die just so God can show His power and glory." However, one must understand that God knew all along that Pharaoh was never going to repent from sin and conceitedness; therefore, God allowed Pharaoh his free will and to die a tragic death amid his sin. God allowed Pharaoh to live out his choices without hindering him, yet with God's will preceding:

Romans 9:14-24

"For He (God) says to Moses, 'I will have mercy on whom I have mercy, and I will have compassion on whom I have compassion.' So then it depends not on human will or exertion, but on God, who has mercy. For the Scripture says to Pharaoh, 'For this very purpose I have raised you up, that I might show my power in you, and that my name might be proclaimed in all the earth.' So then He has mercy on whomever He wills, and He hardens whomever He wills. You will say to me then, 'Why does He still find fault? For who can resist His will?' But who are you, O man, to answer back to God? Will what is molded say to its molder, 'Why have you made me like this?' Has the potter no right over the clay, to make out of

the same lump one vessel for honorable use and another for dishonorable use? What if God, desiring to show His wrath and to make known His power, has endured with much patience vessels of wrath prepared for destruction, in order to make known the riches of His glory for vessels of mercy, which He has prepared beforehand for glory—even us whom He has called, not from the Jews only but also from the Gentiles?" You see, God created us; we did not create Him; therefore, He does not "need us" to exist, and neither does God "need us" for Himself to exist—we need Him. And because we humans, who are so often selfish and sinful, will often deceive ourselves into believing that we don't need God; essentially believing that we exist on our own and came into existence upon our own volition. God created us out of pure love, wanting to share with us His love, His glory, His beauty, and His creation of all things, including His Son. So, you see, there is nothing of God that is selfish; He is nothing but pure incomprehensible love. Once again, to God, the death of our physical body in this world is trivial in comparison to the death of our spirit; remember, we came from dust, and dust we shall return. Therefore, if a person dies from being ill, it is their body that dies and not their actual spirit—their spirit lives on—provided they had accepted Jesus Christ as their Lord and Savior, believing with all their heart, soul, mind, and strength. Which is why God wants us all to relinquish ourselves to Him so that our spirit can live on with Him, for eternity. You see, God is always working behind the scenes, often using situations that appear or seem "horrible" to us are in reality being allowed and even orchestrated by God for our good and for the good of others. But even more, these events are always happening for His glory and for His Kingdom. A perfect example of this was the crucifixion and death of Jesus Christ; which appeared to be horrible and tragic for those who watched and experienced (and it was); however, look what God had in mind all along and look what He brought from it—the Savior of the world. The death of Jesus on the cross was the most loving sacrifice one could ever give; a sacrifice of one's body through brutal torture and death has brought life to many. And though His physical body had perished on the cross (for the time being), His spirit was still with the Father:

Luke 23:46

"Then Jesus, calling out with a loud voice, said, 'Father, into your hands I commit my spirit!'"

Jesus took everything we deserved: torture, abandonment, hell, and death. Had He not, the world would have no chance of being saved from its sin and from eternal condemnation. And though Jesus was perfect and without sin, He paid the ultimate price—a price we ourselves could not pay. He paid our debt, a debt He did not owe and a debt we could not pay. Therefore, you can know for certain that Jesus Christ weeps for us out of anguish, grief, and sorrow for when we in body and spirit have become sick and ill; whether it be sickness and illness derived from our body due to physical illness, or whether it be from spiritual illness derived from our sinful nature. Either way, Jesus weeps for you, just as He did for His beloved friend Lazarus and the others. Which is all the more reason why we need to walk with Jesus in love, faith, trust, and hope, as we turn away from sin and turn to our Lord and Savior who is always with us:

Joshua 1:9

"Have I not commanded you? Be strong and courageous. Do not be frightened, and do not be dismayed, for the LORD your God is with you wherever you go."

Deuteronomy 31:6
"Be strong and courageous. Do not fear or be in dread of them, for it is the LORD your God who goes with you. He will not leave you or forsake you."
Jesus knows what death is like but also knows what it's like to lose a loved one and how difficult it can be. I, myself, have had many people in my life whom I loved pass away suddenly and unexpectedly, and several of them were relatively young. And depending on what I knew about them and depending on my relationship with them, it influenced how I grieved. Because as it were, even those who passed away unexpectedly, I often felt more joy than grief because I knew they loved Jesus and were longing to be with Him and are now with Him in a much better place—a place that can't even be compared to life here on Earth. Therefore, if a loved one passes away from this Earth and you know that they had an intimate and loving relationship with Jesus Christ, then it makes complete sense to have joy and sorrow happening all at once. Thus, joy in knowing that the loved one is truly in a much better place as they are being held in the most loving and peaceful arms of the Father, but sorrow in knowing that you have lost their presence in this world as you loved them dearly and enjoyed living life with them. When two people have a relationship together through the love of God, there is nothing greater or more powerful; because God is Love. God loves us not because of anything we've done or haven't done, but simply because He loves. Whereas, many people will say they love others; however, if their love is not first derived from and through God Himself, then what they have is not true love. Oftentimes, love is mistaken for lust, feelings, emotions, wants, and needs, which can change at any given time. Unfortu-

nately, and all too often, people will "love" others based on their own personal needs and wants; and because it's based on performance, their "love" is fickle. This type of relationship is what would be called a "consumerism" relationship because it's not about what one person can give to the other; it is always about what one person can gain or get from someone else. The fact of the matter is, there are innumerable amounts of people in this world who live within this ideology but are in utter denial of it. If this were not true, then we wouldn't have a world so full of hate, resentment, divorce, murder, theft, envy, and so on. Any relationship that a person has that is not founded on Love (God) is favorable to fail (including marriages), because their relationship is based on emotions, conditions, expectations, and not Love. I once heard a young couple who were struggling in their marriage state that they needed to get back to the "roots" of what brought them together in the first place. What this couple was saying is that they needed to get back to doing the things they did together when they first started dating, which were "fun things," in the idea that it was the "fun things" that made them "love" each other. They were trying to relive their feelings and emotions of lust and excitement. However, it was obvious that this was not what they needed; what was needed and what was missing in their marriage was an intimate relationship with God. This couple's "roots" were not derived from love but were founded on "fun things" (pleasures and emotions), and not the love of God. In a world so consumed by the need for success, now more than ever, people seek to live out their lives independently, even in their marriages. Not only do they not want their spouse or significant other to hinder them from their desires and ambitions, but many will even attempt to make God their servant. They expect God to meet every need and expectation of theirs while never thanking Him for what they already have. So not only do they want God to meet their needs, but they expect others such as their spouse, family, and friends to cater to their very needs as well. This type of thinking will lead to a breakdown within relationships every time, and if nothing changes, it will destroy the relationship permanently because it is not founded first on love:

Philippians 2:3-4

"Do nothing from selfish ambition or conceit, but in humility count others more significant than yourselves. Let each of you look not only to his own interests, but also to the interests of others."

Put yourself in God's "shoes"; imagine being the Creator, who created us for the mere purpose of having a loving and intimate father-childlike relationship with Him, yet is rejected by many of whom He loves and has created. Imagine being a father who, from his children, is only ever acknowledged through wants, desires, and needs, especially when they have become sick, injured, or have found themselves in a state of despair. Imagine the grief and sorrow that God perpetually has from the abuse of those in whom He created to have an intimate relationship with. Moreover, God is often the first to get blamed and even resented when things don't go the way a person expects them to or when something bad happens in their life. Which, this is precisely what the devil wants; the devil wants humanity to spite God for whenever things don't go their way. But when things are going as expected, humanity otherwise has no problem disregarding God; and in doing so, is what I call "The devil's sweet spot." In the next passage you are about to read from the book of Revelation, are words spoken by God Himself to those who use and abuse Him; and will help you better understand what I mean by "The devil's sweet spot":

Revelation 3:15-17

"I know all the things that you do. You are neither hot nor cold. I wish that you were one or the other! But since you are like lukewarm water, neither hot nor cold, I will spit you out of my mouth! You say, 'I am rich. I have everything I want. I don't need a thing!' And you don't realize that you are wretched and miserable and poor and blind and naked."

As you just read, the devil knows that God detests lukewarm "Christians" and even those who may not consider themselves Christians but still look to God in some manner for their own selfish needs. The devil sees how there are many people who ultimately are using God as an objective to meet their needs, and the devil preys on this ideology. Which, in all reality, if a person is attempting to live life "independently" without God but on their own terms, then for all intents and purposes, they are living a life within the Devil's terms. You see, many people have this belief that when they are living "independently" and on "their own terms," they perceive themselves to be doing so with little help from God, but they also believe that they are not under the control of the devil either. Oftentimes, they perceive themselves to be living within this "middle ground" or "common ground" as if they exist and are functioning upon their own volition. And by doing so, they are playing right into the hands of Satan as they have become his marionette, enslaved to his devices. Yet, day after day, many people struggle as they walk in darkness attempting to live within this "middle ground" of "independency," and are doing so to their own peril. Therefore, I call you to be the one who stands firm in Jesus Christ, within His love and righteousness; be the Light that draws others out from darkness. However, be on guard, stay awake, lest you be overcome by darkness yourself. Because "Bad company ruins good people" and "A little leaven leavens the whole lump" (the word leaven translates to spoilage or sin):

Galatians 5:9

"A little leaven leavens the whole lump."

The Apostle Paul describes and lectures about this very thing. Paul says, we who walk in the Light as children of God are not to associate with those who walk in darkness. Although Paul is not saying that we who walk in the Light are to completely disassociate ourselves with those who walk in darkness, but that we are not to have a personal relationship with them in so much as that we start to follow their sinful ways. Paul is also alluding to the idea that it is not for us to "Find the good in people" insomuch as that we are to overlook a person's perpetual sin just so that we can continue to have a personal relationship with them. To the contrary, Paul is expressing that through discernment we are to "judge" those who are living in perpetual sin and to admonish them—more specifically, those who are of the church:

1 Corinthians 5:9-13

"I wrote to you in my letter not to associate with sexually immoral people—not at all meaning the sexually immoral of this world, or the greedy and swindlers, or idolaters, since then you would need to go out of the world. But now I am writing to you not to associate with anyone who bears the name of brother if he is guilty of sexual immorality or greed, or is an idolater, reviler, drunkard, or swindler—not even to eat with such a one. For what have I to do with judging outsiders? Is it not those inside the church whom you are to

judge? God judges those outside. "Purge the evil person from among you."

A common adage, one that most of us have heard or have even said ourselves, is what the Apostle Paul was essentially saying, which is this: "Who you choose to hang around with is likely who you'll become." Therefore, Paul says, "Purge the evil from among you." The mark of a true Christian is not one who is swayed or influenced by others but is otherwise firm and steadfast within the righteousness of Christ. But then there is another idiom that is commonly said and heard amongst humanity, which goes something like this: "Well, I try to find the good in everyone." My initial response or question to the person who is making this statement is, why? Why are you "trying" to find the good in them? You shouldn't have to "try"; whereas, the one who is doing evil is the one who should be "trying." Furthermore, why and when did it become another person's obligation to "find the good" in someone and to overlook their sin just to have a relationship with them—good is good and sin is sin, therefore see it for what it is. If a person is trying to "find the good in everyone," then they for all intents and purposes are attempting to cover up, justify, and even make excuses for another person's sinful actions. Which, by doing so, that person is innately falling into sin themselves as they delude and deprive themselves of truth and reality, while breaking their own personal boundaries that they have for themselves. Which, again, is why the Apostle Paul said, "Purge the evil from among you." In the following passage you are soon to read, are words that were spoken by King David as he relates to the importance of not associating with evil and the necessity to walk in the faithfulness of God:

Psalms 26:3-5

"For your steadfast love is before my eyes, and I walk in your faithfulness. I do not sit with men of falsehood, nor do I consort with hypocrites. I hate the assembly of evildoers, and I will not sit with the wicked."

I, for a good part of my life, adhered to the ideology that it was my obligation to "find the good in everyone" just so that I could say, "I get along with everybody." And as I endeavored to live this out, I eventually, through many difficulties, learned that this conventional line of thinking was nothing more than a detriment to my well-being. Which, at times, came with severe consequences as I often found myself in many peculiar or less-than-ideal situations—situations that would affect me for the rest of my life. Now, don't misconstrue all of what I have been saying up to this point, because, in some manner, we should give every person a chance to become a friend and to show themselves who they truly are without prejudice. Especially if we can be the hands and feet of Jesus that could potentially lead a person out from their sin and darkness. However, relationships should come naturally; especially if the characteristics of everyone involved align with the fruits of the Holy Spirit: which is love, joy, peace, patience, kindness, goodness, faithfulness, gentleness, and self-control. Yes, we all sin and have our faults, but if these characteristics of the Holy Spirit are not what a person is striving for, then any relationship founded on anything else is going to crumble:

1 Corinthians 15:33

"Do not be deceived:"Bad company ruins good morals."

Therefore, I tell you, be wise in your relationships, and if someone is living in ways that don't align with the Holy Spirit, then let them be. If they sin against you, then address the issue with them directly, and if they don't want to confess, apologize, and turn away from their sin, then it is not your obligation to "find the good in them" just so you can maintain a (toxic) relationship with them:

Revelation 22:11

"Let the evildoer still do evil, and the filthy still be filthy, and the righteous still do right, and the holy still be holy."

We Christians should always be looking for opportunities to lead and guide someone out of sin and darkness and into living a better life through a relationship with Jesus Christ. At the beginning of this chapter, we saw how Jesus did this very thing as He used the death of His beloved friend Lazarus to bring many sinners to believing in Him. Jesus often befriended sinners not so He could be like them, but so that the sinners could become like Jesus—He who knew no sin. God promises and tells us that He will remember our sins no more should we turn away from sin and give our lives over to Jesus Christ—through whom we are purified and sanctified. To Him be all the glory, now and forevermore.

Hebrews 8:12

"For I will be merciful to their unrighteousness, and their sins and their iniquities will I remember no more."

WHO GOD THE FATHER IS - WHO HE IS NOT - AND HOW WE ARE TO ABIDE IN HIM

1 Corinthians 8:6
"But for us, there is one God, the Father, by whom all things were created, and for whom we live. And there is one Lord, Jesus Christ, through whom all things were created, and through whom we live."

How does the One and only True Triune God differ from all other "gods?" The short answer is this: Apart from the True Triune God, what other "god" gave up His life so that we as sinners could have eternal life and escape eternal death? Apart from the True Triune God, what other "god" came to Earth carnally, not to be served, but to serve? Apart from the True Triune God, what other "god" says we are saved by His grace and not by "works" —whereas every other "god" says that we must adhere to some sort of "morals" and "ethics" in order to make it into Heaven? Apart from the True Triune God, what other "god" wants to impart to His children His very own glory and inheritance versus keeping it all to Himself? Through His death on a tree, the One and Only True Triune God says to all: repent, come to Me, love Me and accept my Grace, and you will have eternal life in My Kingdom. God being one with His Son Christ Jesus and one with the Holy Spirit is the author of life and is the ultimate deity of what makes up the Holy Trinity. We know that God the Father first and foremost depicts Himself as being a masculine male figure above all else; but we must also see how all femininity & femaleness originate from the nature and being of God as well. We see throughout Scripture how the Godhead has many names or titles: God the Father, Jesus the Christ, the Holy Spirit, King of kings, Lord of lords, Prince of Peace, the I Am, Abba, Elohim, Yahweh, Adonai, Jehovah, Yeshua, El Shaddai, the Father of Light, Father of Glory, and so on. Not because He is many Gods but because He has many characteristics:

Revelation 19:16

"On his robe and on his thigh, he has a name written: King of kings and Lord of lords."

One of the most important aspects to hold in thought as we use these many names or titles that originated from God is that they are Holy and Sacred. We see throughout Scripture and in the world today how many of God's titles have been and are used allegorically to describe people that God has chosen to be His ambassadors. Such as Abraham, who God said would be the "father" of many nations. Even Abraham's wife Sarah who addressed her husband as "lord," or how Jacob referred to his brother Esau as "lord." Not because any of them were actually a Lord (capital L), but because they were representatives of the Lord. The same goes for many who were regarded as kings, such as King David and his son King Solomon; it's not that they were the ultimate kings, but that they were representing God through their kingsmanship. Jesus referred to the devil as being the "father of lies"; Jesus was metaphorically imputing the title of "father" to the devil because the devil himself is the ultimate liar. What must be understood is this: the many titles that are derived from God Himself, that as they are being used to allegorically describe people here on Earth, are never to be used out of context. Might this be one of several reasons why God gave His 3rd commandment which says, "Do not take the Lord's name in vain." Therefore, God is essentially saying, "Do not take and apply in any literal sense any of my many holy, preeminent, and sacred names to any human, creature, man-made object, or to anything here on Earth or in Heaven above." For example: there are various types of clergymen from varying religions who selectively regard themselves as "priests" and "fathers"; addressing themselves in a manner which has no biblical foundation—especially from within the New Testament. The idea of there being any "priests" here on Earth was nullified when Jesus Christ came to Earth in flesh and was made to be the ultimate high priest forever. Yet, we still see mortal men selectively calling themselves "priests" and other related names as they attempt to distinguish themselves from the rest of humanity—as if they were called by God to do so. What is even more perverse about this ideology is how these same men not only want to be regarded as "priests," but they also want to be addressed as "fathers" —as if they are preeminent to all other fathers. One could also make the claim that this concept is even blasphemous; as it was made very clear by God Himself that Jesus had become the "forever High Priest"— "After the order of Melchizedek." While yes, before Christ came to Earth to be the forever High Priest, God would designate specific high priests to be intermediaries between Him and the people and did so for good reason. However, upon Jesus becoming the eternal High Priest, God had also commanded that all who are of the body of Christ have become a "royal priesthood."

Therefore, it is through Jesus that we are all said to be priests—every one of us—not just specific individuals:
Revelation 1:5-6
"And from Jesus Christ, who is the faithful witness, the first-born from the dead, and the ruler of the kings of the earth. To him who loves us and has freed us from our sins by his blood, and has made us to be a kingdom and priests to serve his God and Father—to him be glory and power for ever and ever! Amen"
1 Peter 2:9-10
"But you are a chosen race, a royal priesthood, a holy nation, a people for his own possession, that you may proclaim the excellencies of him who called you out of darkness into his marvelous light. Once you were not a people, but now you are God's people; once you had not received mercy, but now you have received mercy."
Upon Jesus becoming the eternal High Priest in flesh and in Spirit, He became the eternal "bridge" (priest) between humanity and God; more specifically for those who have accepted Jesus Christ as Lord and Savior, believing this with all their heart, soul, mind, and strength. God, unto others, allows and implements titles that would otherwise only pertain to Him, for the mere purpose of displaying and revealing His very own characteristics, His glory, and even Himself to the rest of the world. Therefore, any designation or title that is given by God to any person here on Earth is given for the ultimate glory of God and not for the glory of that person. If you are familiar with the Old Testament: King Saul, who by God was initially made to be a king but was later stripped of his designation as king because he became selfish and corrupt, as he sought after his own glory and abused his power without repentance. This further demonstrates that Jesus Christ

is the One and only true King and that anyone who is not for Him is against Him; and that anyone who is against Him will be destroyed in the process:

Revelation 17:14

"They will make war on the Lamb, and the Lamb will conquer them, for he is Lord of lords and King of kings, and those with him are called and chosen and faithful."

There have been and continue to be many worldly views and ideologies through which people use in their attempt to describe who God is and how He functions within this world. But, for the sake of sanity, I'm going to mention only a few and will do so for edification purposes in the hopes that there may be some enlightenment to follow. First, let's think pragmatically: we know that there are in a range of a billion people that exist here on Earth, and of these billions of people, it's realistic to say that we can't all be right in our individualistic thinking, theories, and beliefs. Therefore, there needs to be a fundamental truth and structure from which all things exist, and without a fundamental structure, things would otherwise naturally self-destruct. For example: look at the juxtaposition between nature and humanity; nature is functioning as was intended—harmoniously living for and praising God within its existence. Whereas humanity, through greed, jealousy, envy, hate, the quest for power and control, etc., is spiraling into its own destruction. This is all occurring not because there is no God or that God has left the world, but because much of humanity has left God. And though it's not because people don't believe in God—because most do—it's due to their relationship with God and how they view God. Many people depict God as this "distant spiritual being" of a "higher power" who essentially "threw together" this planet called Earth. As if God sits in some "far-off place" within the universe doing His own thing while humanity here on Earth endeavors to run the show and fend for itself. For others, God is seen as this all-powerful yet corrupt and angry spiritual being who sits high above in the heavens, overlooking the world and humanity as He looks to smite whomever He can if they don't follow His rules. Moreover, it is also believed and said that God will at times, as often as He chooses, intercede and orchestrate good and bad things to occur all without any real purpose, as if it is all a game to Him. Likewise, many believe that God is just some sort of patriarchal tyrant who is always judging and condemning who He can, as He orchestrates suffering upon those who don't obey Him, His laws, and His commandments. But then, there are many people who are polytheistic; in the idea that there are many gods. Such as a moon god, a sun god, a mountain god, a water god, a wind god, and so on. And though there are many more versions of what people perceive God to be, the final one to mention is likely the most common, which is this: that God is indeed real and that He does in some manner play "some kind" of relational role within the lives of everyone. However, this "some kind" of relational role commonly translates to: people reaching out to God only when they are in need of something or in times of despair. Therefore, it's not until a person has found themselves caught up in some sort of trouble or turbulent times that they then turn to God for help because they are now in a state of despair with nowhere else to go and no one else to turn to. Whether it be a struggling relationship, severe illness, severe physical trauma, severe emotional trauma, addictions, or any other threatening situation where a person no longer feels as if they are in control of their situation. Even then, within these occurrences, they don't necessarily turn to God for the purpose of having a relationship with Him; but only just to use Him—as if He is their personal servant or an assistant to them. And for many, if God doesn't meet the needs and requests of those who call on Him, they will often discard Him through resentment and bitterness, which further affirms that they were only wanting to use Him for His powers of healing, safety, comfort, vengeance, and so on. And though God knows that He is often being used and abused, will in His incomprehensible yet profound love, mercy, and grace, do what is best in every situation and for everyone involved. Because God's most powerful attribute is LOVE:

1 John 4:7-8

"Beloved, let us love one another, for love is from God, and whoever loves has been born of God and knows God. Anyone who does not love does not know God, because God is love."

1 John 4:16

"So, we have come to know and to believe the love that God has for us. God is love, and whoever abides in love abides in God, and God abides in him."

Yes, God is Love; therefore, love is not just another word or term that is simply applied or associated with God as if it is just another sensuality—no, it's way more nuanced than that. You see, love and the power of love simply cannot exist without God, because once again, **God is Love** (literally). Thus, as you just read within the verses, if you don't have God in your heart, then you truly don't have love. You may have within yourself many strong feelings and emotions which can be briefly overwhelming at times, but it is not love. Which is why lust and love are often confused and misunderstood—as if they are one and the same—however, they are not. Lust is essentially a conglomeration of sensualities; however, sensualities such as feelings and emotions are merely just that—feelings and emotions—they come, and they go. However, love—true love (God's Love)—if it is in you, is not transient but is eternal, because it's unconditional. If you were to look up the word **God** in "Heaven's lexicon," the definition of **God** would be this: **LOVE**. Just as if you were to look up the word **Love** in "Heaven's lexicon," the meaning of **Love** would be this: **GOD**. Our comprehension and knowledge of what we humans perceive God's love to be—though it be absolutely wonderful—is incomprehensible to us. Our understanding of God's love would be like us trying to spot an ant swimming in the ocean; it's overwhelming and incomprehensible:

Job 26:14

"These are just the beginning of all that he does, merely a whisper of his power. Who, then, can comprehend the thunder of his power?"

Even now, what we experience of God's incomprehensible love is only just a taste of what is to come, but for now, a taste is all we need. The full power of Jesus' love will come and be felt when we see Him face to face on that most glorious day. You see, God is so deeply involved in our lives that for those who live in Christ Jesus, God calls us His children; as He calls us to come live in His Light (Jesus). So, what does this mean for us? It means that we can fully put our trust in Jesus, and when we do, He transforms us beyond our comprehension. We know that we can trust God with everything because God unequivocally knows us way better than we know ourselves, and why wouldn't He? He created us:

Psalm 139:1-4

"O LORD, you have searched me and known me! You know

when I sit down and when I rise up; you discern my thoughts from afar. You search out my path and my lying down and are acquainted with all my ways. Even before a word is on my tongue, behold, O LORD, you know it altogether."

God the Father says to His children, "I will never leave you nor forsake you" (Deuteronomy 31:6). As it will be for everyone of us, God knows that throughout our lifetime we will have people who will come and go; whether it be those who are in close relation or whether it be those who are not. People will come and go whether it be on good terms or on bad terms; people will leave us, and we will leave people. Most of us have friends or family that we can turn to when circumstances arise; however, none of these people are guaranteed to be around forever. Even a spouse (if you are married) is not going to be around forever; one of you is likely to die before the other (that is, of course, if it doesn't happen simultaneously). Which is all the more reason why God provided us with an everlasting and immovable "Rock"—a "Firm Foundation"—someone who will remain with us forever; while others come and go and are passing away. This "Rock," this "Foundation," is Jesus Christ. He will always remain; His character never changes; He is always constant and consistent in every way, and His love always endures. You see, we all are in need of someone who can mentor and counsel us through every situation and at all times; one whom we can emulate; one who can fill every role within our lives as a Father and a Mother, a Brother and a Sister, a Friend; one who can be with us at all times and in all areas of our life. When a person allows Jesus Christ into their heart, Jesus will become their immovable, unwavering, unconditionally loving, always full of mercy and grace, impartial to justice, always righteous Father, Mother, Brother, Sister, and Friend. Jesus Christ is irreplaceable; He is the One whose "shoes" cannot be filled—not by anyone here on Earth nor in Heaven above. Jesus was the "Rock" that bore us into existence, even before we were brought mortally into this world. He is the One who formed us and wove us together inside our earthly mother's womb. Therefore, I exhort you to be mindful that God had a plan and a purpose for every one of us and did so before we were ever born in flesh and into this world:

Galatians 1:15

"But when he who had set me apart before I was born, and who called me by his grace."

Psalm 139:13-16

"For you formed my inward parts; you knitted me together in my mother's womb. I praise you, for I am fearfully and wonderfully made. Wonderful are your works; my soul knows it very well. My frame was not hidden from you, when I was being made in secret, intricately woven in the depths of the earth. Your eyes saw my unformed substance; in your book were written, every one of them, the days that were formed for me, when as yet there was none of them."

Deuteronomy 32:18

"You were unmindful of the Rock that bore you, and you forgot the God who gave you birth."

Deuteronomy 32:6

"Do you thus repay the LORD, you foolish and senseless people? Is not he your father, who created you, who made you and established you?"

You see, God has left nothing undone in all His creation. God does not start something and not finish it, nor does He start something without preemptively knowing its full purpose—from its beginning, to its end. Neither does God create things just on a whim and neither does He create things out of impulse; we and all creation were intricately and methodically made. He even knows the very number of hairs on our head at all times:

Matthew 10:30

"But even the hairs of your head are all numbered."

Despite God being so intimate with us throughout the entirety of our lives, many people don't experience this intimacy because they don't seek it from God Himself but otherwise seek it in all the wrong places. For many people, God is often perceived to be just some distant "archaic being" who has lived for some "millions to billions" of years (though He has lived forever). And that He created the Earth some "millions to billions" of years ago, along with "some archaic people" to whom He provided the 10 commandments. And much like the dinosaurs that roamed the Earth some supposed "millions" of years ago, it is believed that the bones of these dinosaurs from "millions" of years ago have been somehow preserved for the duration of said "millions" of years. Now, perhaps, I may have just lost you with my interjection of the long-standing dinosaur theory for which most of the world has come to believe. But bear with me, and you will see where I am going with this. Let's think pragmatically here: Most of us are aware of how the most solidified elements here on Earth, such as rock—which can be found above and below the surface of the Earth—erode and deteriorate over time. And as we know, some elements will erode more quickly than others, which is dependent on many factors such as the surrounding environment. However, most people without further question continue to believe that dinosaur bones from "millions" of years ago have been preserved for said duration to this day—despite the fact of knowing that boulders and even mountains (which are made of rock and metal nonetheless) are eroding daily and are diminishing in size. So, I hope by now that you see where I'm going with this and the point I am making. I find it to be very interesting that so many people believe without any further question, thought, or doubt, in the idea that dinosaurs roamed the Earth some "millions" of years ago. And that after some "millions" of years, we are still finding the remains of dinosaurs today. Yet, every day, millions of people without further thought will question the true existence of God, who He is, and what He does. But they will put no further effort or thought into the questioning of man (more specifically science) about their dinosaur theories and ideologies. Because, perhaps maybe, just maybe, dinosaurs did not roam the Earth some "millions" of years ago; but that it was only just several thousand years ago. And perhaps, could it be, that the dinosaurs roamed the Earth with humanity; and that Earth itself has only been around for less than 10,000 years, which is why we find bones of dinosaurs and humans within the same levels of the Earth. Why is it that people are so quick to believe in the knowledge of man, which is so finite and is often biased, skewed, and opinionated? But they are quick to disregard God and the Bible, even though both scripture and God for thousands of years have dramatically changed the lives of billions of people in the most profound and incomprehensible ways. Much like God and the Bible, most people perceive the God-given 10 commandments as some archaic concept that no longer has any further application or meaning. If you were to venture out and conduct your own census, you would quickly find that most people will struggle in their attempt to recite all 10 of the God-given commandments or to even come up with a few of them. This unequivocally shows how self-absorbed and deluded humanity has become as they stray further and further away from God—as most people live by their own preconceived, prefabricated, self-serving ideals of living. Which is why we have a world where people perceive themselves to be God; therefore, they live as if they have created themselves and are sustaining themselves by their very own doing. Intrinsically, this type of thinking produces only one outcome—chaos and disorder—and why wouldn't it, because within this type of mindset, they are innately at odds with the powers of the Divine. Imagine, if for one day a school board was to leave a large group of children to fend for themselves while they are at school; in the idea that they are to operate and sustain a school facility based on their own perceptions, beliefs, knowledge, understanding, feelings, and emotions—without any adult supervision. In just one day, what do you suppose would come of this? Now apply and assimilate this same scenario to conventional society and the ways in which it operates; which is based on its own perceptions, beliefs, biases, feelings, emotions, sensualities, finite knowledge, and understanding. That said, is why God provided humanity with an instruction manual (the Bible) and with the 10 commandments (aka, the moral laws); in the idea that humanity wouldn't otherwise just destroy itself within a short period. Yet, we see this coming to fruition anyway as most of humanity endeavors to disregard not only God and His instruction manual (the Bible) but also His 10 commandments. Therefore, I want to conclude this chapter by providing you with a better understanding of what the 10 commandments are and how they are still relevant to God and us, even today. I have written them in the premise that if I were to ask

Jesus today, if He could in His own words describe to us His expectations of how we should live out His commandments. Based off scripture, this is what I believe Jesus would say:

1. "I am the Lord your God, your only God. I created you along with everything that exists. Therefore, do not make anything or anyone else your God. And if you do turn to other gods, in your rejection of me, I will say to you upon the day of my return— 'I never knew you.' For it is written":

Matthew 7:21-23

"Not everyone who says to me, 'Lord, Lord,' will enter the kingdom of heaven, but the one who does the will of my Father who is in heaven. On that day many will say to me, 'Lord, Lord, did we not prophesy in your name, and cast out demons in your name, and do many mighty works in your name?' And then will I declare to them, 'I never knew you; depart from me, you workers of lawlessness.'"

2. "And, just as you are not to have any other gods before me, do not idolize anyone or anything before me either; because whatever you idolize over me, for all intents and purposes, has become your god. Therefore, if you idolize money or success, it becomes your god, while you become enslaved to it. Thus, the false god to which you are enslaved, will not save you from eternal destruction. For it is written":

Exodus 22:20

"Whoever sacrifices to any god other than the Lord must be destroyed."

3. "Do not take My name in vain and use it towards anything false, negative, dark, or evil. For I Am infallible, I Am pure, I Am holy, I Am righteous, I Am truth, I Am justice, I Am good, I Am peace, I Am Love, I Am everything but evil. I have no evil in Me; therefore, do not label Me or use My name in any manner that associates Me with evil. I am the Light of the world and of all creation. I and darkness do not get along. For it is written":

Mark 3:28-29

"Truly I tell you, people can be forgiven all their sins and every slander they utter, but whoever blasphemes against the Holy Spirit will never be forgiven; they are guilty of an eternal sin."

4. "Keep the Sabbath day holy, because I am holy. And it's not just about physical rest, but is even more so about spiritual rest. I created the world and everything in it; therefore, every day is holy—because I Am in it. So, stop bickering over what day is to be considered the Holy Sabbath day; you should be finding rest in Me every day and not just one day a week. Besides, how do you know if Saturday will come? How do you know if you will even be alive for the next Sabbath? Therefore, find rest in Me today—tomorrow is not promised, but I Am. For it is written":

Matthew 12:8

"For the Son of Man is Lord of the Sabbath."

5. "Honor me in everything as your ultimate Father and Mother. I Am the One who bore you even before you were born into this world. I Am the One who comforts you and loves you unconditionally. I Am the One who protects you. I Am the One who sustains you and provides you with everything you need. I Am the One who decides whether you will come to Me and into My kingdom eternally, or whether you are to be condemned eternally because you did not love Me and believe in Me with all your heart, soul, mind, and strength. For it is written":

John 3:16-18

"For God so loved the world, that he gave his only Son, that whoever believes in him should not perish but have eternal life. For God did not send his Son into the world to condemn the world, but in order that the world might be saved through him. Whoever believes in him is not condemned, but whoever does not believe is condemned already, because he has not believed in the name of the only Son of God."

Now, for the last five of the 10 commandments. Jesus says (again, paraphrasing), "For I give you these final 5 commandments; I am to be honored through them all as well":

6. "Do not murder; and aside from literal murder, if in your heart you are harboring hate and resentment towards anyone without forgiveness, you essentially have committed murder. For it is written":

1 John 3:15

"Everyone who hates his brother is a murderer, and you know that no murderer has eternal life abiding in him."

7. "Do not commit adultery; for I tell you, take heed, just as it is written in Matthew 5:28":

Matthew 5:28

"But I say to you that everyone who looks at a woman (or man) with lustful intent has already committed adultery with her (or him) in his (or her) heart."

8. "You shall not steal; anything, from anyone. Even if your depraved taxation system is cheating and stealing from you, let them; they are condemning themselves by doing so; don't become a part of their evil schemes by doing in return what they are doing unto you. Even so, if you are withholding your money and not paying what is required of you in taxes, this is theft; not only is it theft but you are also lying, and lying for gain. For it is written":

Proverbs 16:8
"Better to have little, with godliness, than to be rich and dishonest."
Proverbs 19:1
"Better is a poor person who walks in his integrity than one who is crooked in his speech and is a fool."
Mark 12:17
"Jesus said to them, 'Render to Caesar the things that are Caesar's, and to God the things that are God's.' And they marveled at him."

9. "You shall not lie; about anything, or bear false witness (gossip) about anyone. If you do, it will be seen and heard by your Father in heaven—who hears and sees everything. And though you may think that you are getting away with it at the time, it is not so; because no matter how small or big the lie, there are implications; you just may not always see or recognize them. For it is written":
Proverbs 19:5
"A false witness will not go unpunished, and he who breathes out lies will not escape."
Proverbs 19:9
"A false witness will not go unpunished, and he who breathes out lies will perish."

10. "You shall not covet; what does this mean? It means that you shall not want, envy, or lust for what anyone else has. So stop comparing yourself and your life to others. You are not them, and they are not you. For I have every one of you on a different path in life. So stop trying to be like others. You will never have what everyone else has, and the harder you try, the less likely you will obtain it. Chasing after the world and chasing after what everyone else has is like chasing after the wind—it will never be caught. Furthermore, the more you chase after the world and what everyone else has, the more miserable you will be. Therefore, seek Me and live your life for Me, and as you do, I will provide you with everything you need. Most importantly, you will always have my unconditional love, and when you have My love, you will have everything you need":

James 4:2

"You desire and do not have, so you murder. You covet and cannot obtain, so you fight and quarrel. You do not have, because you do not ask (God)."

So, you see, the 10 commandments were given to us for our own good; to keep us on the right path as we endure within a world that is not our ultimate home. If we abide in Jesus, we will naturally abide in His commandments too, and not by our own works or doing but because He is working within us. However, if we try to do things within our own power, we impede the natural power of the Holy Spirit and His ability to work within us. Thus, anything we attempt to change through our own willpower will not last but will only be ephemeral. Jesus Christ, the One who created us, is the only One who can permanently transform us. A true test of whether someone has been transformed by the Holy Spirit versus someone who attempts to transform themselves upon their own willpower is seen by the way they respond upon being tested with trials and tribulations. Therefore, upon being tested, do they respond by defaulting to their old habits and ways or do they respond in a completely different manner —a manner that aligns with the fruits and characteristics of the Holy Spirit? While yes, most change can and will often be gradual, but if the change is perpetually fickle, then it likely has not occurred by the help of and through the works of the Holy Spirit. So you see, Jesus Christ and

His commandments are alive and active and have the power to transform; therefore, whoever gives their life over to Him will be born again—into a new life and into a new family. Blessed be the name of Jesus Christ—forever and ever more. Amen!

Romans 2:12-16

"For all who have sinned without the law will also perish without the law, and all who have sinned under the law will be judged by the law. For it is not the hearers of the law who are righteous before God, but the doers of the law who will be justified. For when Gentiles, who do not have the law, by nature do what the law requires, they are a law to themselves, even though they do not have the law. They show that the work of the law is written on their hearts, while their conscience also bears witness, and their afflicting thoughts accuse or even excuse them on that day when, according to my gospel, God judges the secrets of men by Jesus Christ."

GIVE UP A LIFE OF LIVING FOR YOURSELF FOR A LIFE OF HONOR-ING GOD AND OTHERS IN HUMILITY

Galatians 6:3
"For if anyone thinks he is something, when he is nothing, he deceives himself."
Which is it? Is it that we live in a world full of good people with some otherwise very evil people, or do we live in an evil world with some very good people? Or is it neither of these? Before the Lord blessed me with eyes to see and with ears to hear and before I met Jesus, let me tell you what I perceived at the time and is what conventional society teaches and enables. The common riff goes something like this: "Well, there are "good" people in the world and then there are "bad" people in the world, but I'm "good." Those who are "bad" do the very "bad" things like murder, rape, theft, exploit, and so on; and when they get caught, it makes them even more "bad," whereas had they not been caught, well then they wouldn't be as "bad." And despite the very "bad" people who do the very "bad" things, us "good" people otherwise live in a "good" world where I myself make up the "good" portion—even though we all lie, cheat, steal, lust, hate, judge, gossip, self-serve, and so on." But the common riff doesn't just end there, it continues and goes something like this: "Though bad things are happening in other areas or other cities or that country over there—things such as war, genocide, theft, rape, rioting, and so on—I'm "good" and "comfortable" over here; having everything I need as I live my "good"

and “comfortable” life. So, unless those bad things that are happening elsewhere begin to affect me here where I am, I have no need to care or worry, because I’m a “good” person and only “bad” things happen to “bad” people.” So, as you see, this is the reality of the world we live in, and the Bible speaks all about it. And though we may not always hear people speak these very thoughts and words aloud, you can hear them being said every day if you just listen. Therefore, one must come to terms with and see how utterly conceited, ignorant, naive, selfish, and deceptive these very common lines of thinking are in order to move away from them. However, for the many that do continue to ignore and to live according to these common ideologies, they eventually find themselves amidst difficulties which often leave them confounded and with no other option but to eventually face reality. And so now this “good” person acts as if the world has “come against them” —as they have now become “victimized” by the world. Thus, it is now “the world’s fault” and/or “Gods fault” for the predicament they have found themselves in. This common scenario is profoundly prevalent and is almost always preceded by pride, arrogance, and ignorance. Which is precisely what the devil wants; Satan wants people to be blind and deaf to not only who they are as a person and the evil that is in the hearts of humanity, but then also to who he is and how he functions within this world. Jesus Himself described the devil as being the “father of lies” because it was the devil who introduced deceit into the hearts of humanity. Jesus, during His ministry here on Earth, made this vociferous statement to the Pharisees who were known to be liars and hypocrites as they often misguided people based on lies and deceit, and did so for their own self-preservation:

John 8:44
"You are of your father the devil, and your will is to do your father's desires. He was a murderer from the beginning, and does not stand in the truth, because there is no truth in him. When he lies, he speaks out of his own character, for he is a liar and the father of lies."
Matthew 23:27-28
"Woe to you, scribes and Pharisees, hypocrites! For you are like whitewashed tombs, which outwardly appear beautiful, but within are full of dead people's bones and all uncleanness. So, you also outwardly appear righteous to others, but within you are full of hypocrisy and lawlessness."
If you are unfamiliar with the passages above and are unsure of what to appropriate from them, then let me further expound on them because they very much correlate with contemporary societal ideologies. The passages you just read speak to many people of this world who in their own mind perceive themselves to be self-righteous ("good") —in the idea that they are not sinners—though we all are. In contemporary terms, this person would be described as one who is narcissistic or hubristic as they look down upon others while basking in their own deception of self-perceived moralistic righteousness. They often seek power and control as they live to be praised and validated by others. However, as Jesus said, they are the "walking dead" because they do not live by what they preach; hence the description of them being "full of dead people's bones" and "being unclean" —as was stated by Jesus. The need for power and control was conceived first by Adam and Eve when they were enticed with it by the devil in the Garden of Eden. Jesus spoke vociferously about this as He stated what was to come for those who are self-righteous; as they live for this world chasing

after power, control, money, success, and the many other things this fleeting world has to offer:

John 12:25-26

"Anyone who loves their life will lose it, while anyone who hates their life in this world will keep it for eternal life. Whoever serves me must follow me; and where I am, my servant also will be. My Father will honor the one who serves me."

During Jesus' ministry here on earth, even the disciples of Jesus were at one point becoming prideful, arrogant, and self-righteous as they began to argue about who was the greatest among them. Jesus of course hears their dispute and quickly admonishes them:

Luke 22:24-30

"A dispute also arose among them, as to which of them was to be regarded as the greatest. And he said to them, 'The kings of the Gentiles exercise lordship over them, and those in authority over them are called benefactors. But not so with you. Rather, let the greatest among you become as the youngest, and the leader as one who serves. For whom is the greater, one who reclines at table or one who serves? Is it not the one who reclines at table? But I am among you as the one who serves.'"

God makes it very clear that when it comes to status here on Earth, we as humans are all equal in the sense that not one person is preeminent to another. Much like the passage you just read, Jesus says again that whoever wants to be great must be a servant of all:

Matthew 20:25-28

"But Jesus called them to him and said, 'You know that the rulers of the Gentiles lord it over them, and their great ones exercise authority over them. It shall not be so among you. But whoever would be great among you must be your servant, and whoever would be first among you must be your slave, even as the Son of Man came not to be served but to serve, and

to give his life as a ransom for many.'"

Commonly, people will attempt to cover up their sinful, selfish, and evil nature by putting on a "mask" as they endeavor to conceal their true identity. Although for some, they will put on a "mask" for the purpose of protecting themselves as they attempt to cover up their insecurities and weaknesses, but even more so, to protect themselves from further hurt or harm of others. Today's societal-conventional thinking wants everyone to believe that they need to be "mentally tough" —no matter the cost; the premise is to not display any sort of humility, meekness, or weakness, even if it costs them their life. Because "dying strong" with a "legacy" is more important than anything. This ongoing deception and illusion has misguided so many people from the truth; but even more so from who they were truly created to be as a servant and child of the Most High God. Thus, instead, what we have now are many lost people (souls) who wonder about wearing various types of "masks" depicting to be "mentally tough" —masks that are nothing more than facades of pride, arrogance, and insecurities. And unfortunately, many of these masks of "mental toughness" of which many have come to wear have led to bullying, intimidation, selfishness, greed, envy, jealousy, hate, lies, exploitation, and so on; all of which show what truly lies behind the mask and in the heart of these many people. Because for many people, it is much "easier" for them to put on a daily mask of "mental toughness" than to face their own weaknesses, insecurities, demons, darkness, and who they truly are as a person. Whereas, if a person wants to truly become who God created them to be—as a person of authenticity, they must first face the reality of who they are by putting off their various types of masks.

Which does take intentionality and is a lifelong daily process of introspection, self-control, growth, learning, and most importantly of all, humility. Without humility, a person will often remain lost and disconnected from reality and themselves because their pride distorts everything, which, left unchecked, only leads to self-destruction and spiritual death:

Ezekiel 33:13

"Though I say to the righteous that he shall surely live, yet if he trusts in his righteousness and does injustice, none of his righteous deeds shall be remembered, but in his injustice that he has done, he shall perish."

Because we live in a world where most people seek and want instant gratification, most do not truly obtain what is otherwise known as true mental strength, simply because they do not want to put in the time and effort of what it takes to achieve it. Thus, they disable, defeat, and deprive themselves of their ability to develop true mental strength. Which, truth be told, can only be obtained through a relationship with Jesus Christ, in humility. Oftentimes, for those who are endeavoring to display "mental toughness," they feel that they must be "loud" in their speech and in their presentation, and will do so as a means to compensate and cover for their insecurities. Whereas, if they are not "loud" in their presentation and in their speech, then to them and to conventional society, they are perceived to be "weak." And for those who are more "softer-spoken," they are often perceived to be "weak" —as they tend to mind their own affairs and not allow the trivial things of this world to affect them. Moreover, the softer-spoken people are commonly the ones who can often communicate and present themselves in a more self-controlled manner through humility, genuineness, and authenticity. Because they don't feel the need to be loud, aggressive, controlling, and forceful in order to accomplish their objectives:

1 Thessalonians 4:11-12

"Aspire to live quietly, and to mind your own affairs, and to work with your hands, as we instructed you, so that you may walk properly before outsiders and be dependent on no one."

Was Jesus ever aggressively loud, controlling, or forceful? He was often very direct, concise, and was even at times indignant, but He never demonstrated aggression in the way of being forceful, controlling, or excessively loud towards any specific person or group. Yes, there are times when we are to speak up, but then there are times when we are to just keep quiet; however, there is never a time when we are to be uncontrollably loud, forceful, or aggressive. Now, let me be clear and practical here: because yes, there are many situations in life that require people to be aggressive, forceful, loud, etc.: such as those who are in law enforcement, the military, healthcare, etc., where people have to be subdued, apprehended, etc., because people's lives are at risk. Even civilians have to at times be aggressive or forceful in order to protect the lives of others and themselves. But outside of life-and-death situations, aggression of the various types is usually not warranted. What is also common amongst those who are often uncontrollably loud, or aggressive, controlling, and forceful, is that they have no problem in developing the skill to speak loudly over others—without listening—as they interrupt others while they are still talking. Thus, they lack the self-awareness and the self-control to demonstrate control over their own tongue, words, and actions:

James 3:6

"Among all the parts of the body, the tongue is a flame of fire. It is a whole world of wickedness, corrupting your entire body. It can set your whole life on fire, for it is set on fire by hell itself."

It is really quite simple when it comes to speech: if what you speak are words of truth, encouragement, joy, gratitude, grace, love, mercy, or words of concern for the betterment of others and the greater good, then speak them and do it with sincere humility. However, if your words are not spoken for any of said reasons, then don't speak at all and just hold your tongue. People often will say, "Well, I only speak truth" —as they lie and pontificate about things that hold no truth, and do so based on their own conjured-up beliefs, perspectives, and agendas. Whereas, what a person ought to be asking themselves before they speak: is what I am saying based on facts and real events, or is it based on my own perspectives, biases, opinions, feelings, and emotions, all of which are derived from my own lack of understanding, narrow-mindedness, and pride? In many circumstances, I have witnessed people who speak of others as being "weak" and/or "passive," yet these very same people will have for themselves no personal boundaries of their own with very little self-control. Moreover, these very same people are often enslaved to many addictions, vices, and other coping mechanisms with which they use to ignore their very own issues and insecurities. Oftentimes, these very people will be the first to gossip, hate, judge, envy, and devalue those who do have the ability to display self-control through humility and meekness. Nevertheless, this is often a telltale sign of someone who is truly "weak." Though, I will admit, before I gave my life to Jesus, I also, like many others, was arrogant, ignorant, and prideful, thinking of others as being "weak." When in all reality they were just humble, loving, and kind: and many of them were living a very tough life. Sure, could I blame others and conventional society itself for enabling and teaching me this ideology, yes I could. However, we all reach a point in our lives when our lies and excuses for our actions no longer get us by; as we can no longer blame others, society, or even the devil, for our actions. Because no matter how much we attempt to delude ourselves and others, in the end, truth and reality will always confront us—darkness will always be brought to light. And when it does, this is where we have a life-changing decision to make; and the decision we choose can either make or break us. Commonly, a sign of spiritual maturity is when a person no longer blames anything or anyone, or even their past, present, and even the future, for their ongoing problems, choices, and actions in life. But instead, chooses to live life in humility. When we live life in humility, we function from a place of inner strength and power; and that inner strength and power is Jesus Christ—The Holy Spirit—God the Father:

2 Corinthians 12:10

"For the sake of Christ, then, I am content with weaknesses, insults, hardships, persecutions, and calamities. For when I am weak, then I am strong."

You see, humility cannot be taken from you; you can only give it up. When you function from a place of humility, it allows you to negate actions, words, or thoughts that may otherwise be derived from conceit, personas, agendas, motives, and false expectations—especially ones of superiority and comparison. Humility keeps us grounded in truth and in reality, which allows us to be truthful and real with ourselves and others. Without humility, you will often find yourself living in fear as you attempt to people-please, impress, compare, judge; in an attempt to validate yourself because you are not meeting your own expectations and the expectations of others. Whereas, in humility, you innately become more grateful for who you are as a person and for what God has already given you in life—whether it be big or small—little or much. Either way, you will be grateful and content because you will be without the need to compete against others and the world around you. As for myself, in my daily venture to seek the spiritual power that comes through humility, there is an interesting concept that I have come to discover as I interact with various types of people who perceive humility as a sign of "weakness." I will capitulate myself to the powers of humility ("weakness" to them), and by doing so, the proclivity for them is to let their guard down because they no longer perceive me as a "threat" but as "weak." Thus, as I reside within the powers of humility, such people will often feel as if they are preeminent, therefore, exposing their true identity, good or bad. Though, this is not always easy because my natural human instinct wants to defend myself; however, I can usually stave off that instinct by turning the situation over to God. Knowing that if someone does take advantage of me and my humility, they will be held accountable, by God:

Romans 12:19

"Beloved, avenge not yourselves, but leave it to the wrath of God; for it is written, vengeance is mine, I will repay says the Lord."

Galatians 6:7

"Do not be deceived: God is not mocked, for whatever one sows, that will he also reap."

Therefore, if there be any wrongdoing against me,

whether it be minute or momentous, the Lord will rectify the situation. It may not be in a manner of what one might expect, but it will be dealt with. And though it often appears that those who live in perpetual sin seemingly live life with having little to no issues or ramifications to their actions, it is certain that there are and will be consequences; we just don't always see them. However, keep in mind, the same goes for you; every sin of yours will not be just simply disregarded—even if you are a child of the Most-High God and are cleansed by the blood of Jesus Christ. Because though you are forgiven by the ever-loving, merciful, and gracious Heavenly Father, He will still correct you and rectify the situation—remember, God shows no partiality. Not only have I experienced God's impartiality within my own life, but I have witnessed innumerable accounts of where someone for all intents and purposes had "reaped what they had sown." Oftentimes, these recompenses or indemnifications by God will occur within a short period of time or will occur many years later; I have seen it happen both ways. Either way, it's up to God on how he wants to handle the situation. Therefore, strive to live in the righteousness of Christ; be wise in your words and in your actions because what you say and what you do matters:

Luke 12:2-3

"Nothing is covered up that will not be revealed or hidden that will not be known. Therefore, whatever you have said in the dark shall be heard in the light, and what you have whispered in private rooms shall be proclaimed on the housetops."

Science has only but scratched the surface of its understanding of the human mind concerning its capacity, capabilities, and the many ways in which it functions; whether it be the conscious mind or the unconscious mind. Furthermore, beyond what is tangible, to say that the human mind can be understood is to say that we in some capacity have come to comprehend our Creator—which is impossible. Therefore, the second a person allows their pride and arrogance to distort their judgment of truth and reality is when they have already begun to walk down the arduous path in becoming humbled without choice. Thus, it is often most conducive to a person's overall well-being when they, upon their own volition, can humble themselves, versus being humbled by the powers of divinity:

Matthew 23:12

"Whoever exalts himself will be humbled, and whoever humbles himself will be exalted."

We often hear people use the word "mastery," which can often be used synonymously with the word "perfection" to describe one's achievements, abilities, and talents in who they've become or with what they have accomplished. Mastery is often used cohesively in the description of a vocational title such as a "master" technician or a "master" painter or a "master" chef. Many gurus will tout the word "mastery" as they attempt to encourage someone to "master their craft" to "master their emotions" to "master their money" or to "master who they are." All of which are nothing more than false realities and facades that lead and misguide people into a world of illusions and delusions. We all have our own strengths and weaknesses, gifts and talents; however, even with our strengths, gifts, and talents, we are still limited and finite to what we can do. Furthermore, God is the One who decides whether we are to surpass our limitations or even the limitations of others, and to what extent; either way, if He chooses for us to do so, it will always be for His purpose and His glory, and not our own. According to several lexicons, "Mastery" is defined as: "having or acquiring complete control and/or knowledge of something." In other words, "mastery" means to have something "perfected" —to be "perfect" —to be "flawless." Which, for someone to say that they have "perfected" or "mastered" something, is about as logical and practical as saying that we humans here on Earth can live without air, which is impossible. Yet, many people legitimately believe that "mastery" and "perfection" are achievable—and many believe they have it—that is, until they lose it. If someone was ever wanting to set themselves up to fail or to feel like a failure, then adhering to the premise that "mastery" or "perfection" is achievable, and would be the first step down that arduous path to failure and disappointment—especially if one is conceited enough to believe it. We all have seen or have heard, and have likely even done it ourselves through pride and arrogance, boasted about something that was accomplished or obtained. Overtly, we see this most predominantly in the arena of worldwide sports, where there is always one athlete that is touted to be the "best." Oftentimes, it is the athlete themselves who will boast of themselves as being the "best" —insinuating that they are the "master of their craft"; that they have "perfected" who they are and what they do—in essence superior to all others. But then without fail, as it always goes, eventually another athlete comes along and smashes the record and stats of that athlete—and sometimes even the athlete themselves. This occurrence is not just segregated to the world of sports; we see this take place in every profession, vocation, and in everyday life. Moreover, what we often see when one person becomes defeated by another is how their pride and arrogance manifests and morphs into envy, jealousy, hate, judgment, resentment, contempt, and so on as their records and egos become smashed. Even more, they will often become bitter and resentful not only towards themselves, but even God. Thus, what one should be seeking is not that of "mastery" or "perfection"; but in humility, striving for results that lead them into living a life of honoring God by using their God-given gifts and talents to serve Him and others, and not themselves. The biggest lie the devil tells people is that he doesn't exist; and that we have no need for God because we can do everything on our own. I, in my younger years of life, unwittingly disregarded the idea of there being a devil, mainly because the devil was never talked about (which is common here in the Western world). Instead, I adhered to the premise that God was the cause of all my troubles; therefore, like many, I directed my anger towards God. And by doing so, I, like many others, was a marionette playing right into the devil's schemes. As one might say, "Unless you have had a run-in with the devil, you and the devil are likely heading in the same direction"; which I tell you, this is not a good thing. And if you are questioning as to whether you have or have not ever had a "run-in" with the devil, I assure you, you will certainly know when you have. However, if you don't think you have, you may want to ponder diligently about the life you are living and the path in which you are on. At minimum, I implore you to adjudicate your beliefs and perceptions of who the devil is and how he functions within this world—read the Bible and learn. For myself, it wasn't until I had personally experienced through others, such evil; then realizing the reality of the devil's existence and the evil that resides within us all. Moreover, at the same time further realizing how much I needed Jesus; that without Him, I am helpless and defenseless in my fight against not only the devil himself, but the evil that resides within me and in others. Once again, it's not until a person can fully acknowledge and face the truth and reality that we all have evil in our hearts; then will a person no longer be walking the same path as the devil and can start fighting for their life by walking in the Light of Jesus Christ, allowing the Holy Spirit to work within by transforming our hearts:

1 John 1:7-10

"But if we walk in the light, as he is in the light, we have fellowship with one another, and the blood of Jesus his Son cleanses us from all sin. If we say we have no sin, we deceive ourselves, and the truth is not in us. If we confess our sins, he is faithful and just to forgive us our sins and to cleanse us from all unrighteousness. If we say we have not sinned, we make him a liar, and his word is not in us."

Most people have no problem pointing out how flawed others are or how evil and corrupt the world is; however, when it comes to pointing this out about themselves, many would rather die (literally) than face the truth and acknowledge it—as pride and ignorance get in the way of truth. And because they have been ignoring the truth for so long, when they do get badly hurt by another sinner, they have a difficult time forgiving and loving them because their anger and bitterness enslaves them. Which almost always leads to resentment; and oh, how deadly resentment is for the soul. As some of you have probably heard: for the one who is resenting, resentment is like ingesting poison as they wait for the one who they are resenting to die. Let me put it another way: harboring resentment is like drinking a glass of poison day after day, and while you wait for the one who has wronged you to die, you are the one who will be slowly dying inside. So, as a person continues to toil in their ongoing frustration, anger, and bitterness (aka resentment) towards another person, they are not only damaging themselves physiologically and psychologically, but will be destroying themselves even more so spiritually. If you are not aware of how resentment destroys physiologically, psychologically, and spiritually, let me briefly elaborate to provide you with further insight into how it does. Stress alone is the precursor to many different types of diseases such as cancer, heart disease, diabetes, high blood pressure, obesity, and so much more. When we heavily stress over things for extended periods of time, stress disrupts the many normal functions within the body. Because when we stress, the body releases certain types of hormones and other harmful chemicals that are not good for the mind or body—aside from the fact that most people tend to eat unhealthy when they stress as well. And when a certain kind of hormone is being released too often, too little, or too much, it can cause significant damage to the cells themselves and your organs overall. This is why it is said that harboring resentment is like ingesting poison; because it truly does equate to the slow poisoning of one's body—causing irreversible physiological damage. To simplify, the psychological aspect coincides with the physiological aspect as well as the spiritual aspect—as it leads to many unhealthy thoughts and actions. However, the death of one's physical body does not necessarily equate to spiritual death, but it has the potential—which is far more of a concern than that of physical death. When we choose resentment over forgiveness, humility, and love, we are essentially denying God's ability to be in control and make things right; but even more, you are denying the fact that Jesus died on the cross not only for your sins but for the sins of the person whom you are resenting. Thus, for all intents and purposes, you are insinuating that your knowledge, wisdom, and understanding is superior to that of God, as you attempt to handle the situation on your own through resentment and vengeance. What a person must come to understand is that as they harbor resentment and judgment upon others, by doing so, they are also bringing judgment upon themselves. For God Himself said: you must forgive others of their sin, so that you may be forgiven by God of your sin:

Matthew 6:14

"For if you forgive others their trespasses, your heavenly Father will also forgive you, but if you do not forgive others their trespasses, neither will your Father forgive your trespasses."

So, you see, unless a person forgives whomever they are resenting, not only is God Himself not going to forgive them of their sins; but that it will be to their own peril as they lead themselves to spiritual death—which is eternal death. Consider this: resentment is likened to hate, and here is what Jesus said about hate:

1 John 3:15

Anyone who hates a brother or sister is a murderer, and you know that no murderer has eternal life residing in him.

Therefore, a person cannot love and hate at the same time; there is no room for both, not for those who are in Christ Jesus. Remember, God shows no partiality; you are a sinner just as much as the next person, which includes the person whom you are resenting or hating. I, like many others in the world, have been lied to, hurt, and betrayed, even by those who are supposed to be trustworthy, such as family and friends. Forgiving those who have hurt us is not always easy and often does take time to heal; however, forgiveness must be given, and it must be done so with purity and sincerity. Because if you find yourself forgiving out of obligation or simply because you feel "it is the right thing to do," then your forgiveness is done in vain and holds no value. "Conditional forgiveness" is no different than "conditional love"; it's futile and holds no value. There is no partiality about this matter—either you love someone, or you don't—there is no in-between. Thus, you cannot partially love someone just as you cannot partially forgive someone; love is love—forgiveness is forgiveness. We often hear people say something like: "Well, I love so and so when they treat me right and are good to me, but because sometimes they do this or do that and upset me, it makes me not love them." Anyone who makes this type of statement is only fooling themselves; because what they are describing is not love, this would be "conditional love" —which as I said, in reality, is not love at all. "Conditional love" is nothing more than utter pride and selfishness; because it's merely predicated upon the other person's performance. Okay, so how do we stop poisoning ourselves through resentment or through the "conditional love" ideology? Do we just simply stop resenting and forgive? If it were only that easy, right? Unfortunately, because we are human and imperfect, many in a futile attempt will try to eliminate, mitigate, or drown their resentment away through addictions and distractions such as food, alcohol, drugs, sex, and so on. Many people will bury themselves in their work or career in order to distract themselves from facing the truth and reality of their situation, which of course only makes things worse. Because as a person endeavors to shove down deep their hurtful experiences in an attempt to ignore them, it only amplifies the situation as they perpetuate the cycle. And as a result, this often causes even more resentment. Therefore, it is essential for a person to confront the root cause of their resentment or their "conditional love" mentality sooner rather than later; so they can process their experience or trauma in a healthy manner while mending relationships at the same time. Most people believe that if they just "give it time," or "space" their hurt will just heal and dissipate on its own, which will then allow them to forgive. However, that's not how it works, and is why so many people have a hard time forgiving or why many people never do forgive. Which is why so many people continue to harbor resentment unto death. The most crucial aspect of overcoming resentment is this: a person must first forgive, in order for them to heal; that is the order in which it must occur—forgive first, then heal—if it does not occur in this order then they will never forgive, because healing comes through forgiveness. Consider this: Jesus, who was ridiculed, betrayed, tortured, and persecuted in nearly every way and by so many, did not resent but instead immediately forgave—even before going to the cross and enduring all that He did. Not only did Jesus forgive immediately, He gave His life up as a ransom; for not only those who hated Him and betrayed Him, but even for the rest of the world of sinners. Jesus didn't wait for time to pass so that His hurt could heal; no, He immediately forgave so that He could heal not Himself, but the world. You see, as a person harbors resentment, it is crucial to recognize that aside from the hurt they are experiencing, much of what a person is oftentimes feeling—is simply just that—feelings and emotions. Which often equates to and is derived from sorrowful pride (aka, woe is me, I'm the victim); and is why it turns into resentment. However, these feelings and emotions don't have to control a person. Hurt cannot be controlled, but a person can to some capacity gain control over their feelings and emotions—their pride. Which is oftentimes what holds a person back from forgiving; it's not their hurt that hinders them, but their pride. What's the antidote for pride; humility and love. Oftentimes, when people resent, they will involve themselves in the lives and/or marital lives of others by meddling and gossiping; which truth be told, upon doing so, it is not uncommon that they find themselves amidst the very troubles they were gossiping over, such as divorce. Because, again, truth be told—Galatians 6:7: "you reap what you sow" —is all the more reason to let go of resentment, bitterness, gossip, comparison, and pride:

Ecclesiastes 4:4

"Then I saw that all toil and all skill in work come from a man's envy of his neighbor. This also is vanity and a striving after wind."

Lastly, aside from forgiveness needing to happen first, what must be understood regarding the person who wronged another is that the person who wronged them had to first allow the hurt that they endured from someone else to lead them to the choice of acting out and to hurt yet another person. Therefore, in order for the last person to hurt the previous person, the current person had to first give up their own dignity, self-respect, boundaries, and self-control, allowing themselves to carry out their actions against another person. That said, if such a person lacks the self-control to even respect themselves, why would it be primitive to think that they wouldn't hurt anyone else along the way? So you see, it's a perpetual cycle, and the only way the cycle can be negated is if someone along the way chooses to forgive through love and humility. Think of it this way: Hypothetically, let's say you were to become resentful towards a toddler because the toddler disrespected you, but because it is a toddler, you know that they have yet to learn what respect is much less what it even means to have self-respect. Thus, it would be irrational of you to resent this toddler, right? —yes, of course, because it's a toddler. Now apply this situation to an adult, where many adults function like toddlers because the adult has neglected to hold themselves accountable by turning away from their childish and selfish ways. Therefore, in most circumstances, to harbor resentment towards another adult is like harboring resentment towards a toddler because both the toddler and the immature adult lack the maturity to own up to their actions and to apologize for their wrongdoing. However, on the other hand, if a person has hurt you and has confessed and apologized to you for their wrongdoings, but you are still harboring resentment, then you must face the fact that you are the one who is being immature. Moreover, if you are harboring resentment towards someone and have not yet moved on through forgiveness, it could also be that you are wanting more validation from this person than what you rationally deserve. Because if you weren't doing this, you wouldn't continue to be so bothered by them. But because you are continuously bothered by them (though they have apologized), you essentially want them to provide you with further acknowledgment or validation of you being the "victim" — you want to feel superior. You want further validation in knowing that they are feeling shame and guilt for what they had done to you. Which by the way, you are then crossing the threshold of becoming sadistic. This would be again, another example of pride; because, while yes you may be the "victim" of a wrongdoing but at the same time you are essentially wanting to feel superior to that person, and you want them to feel inferior to you. Consider this: what if the person who hurt or wronged you was to die tomorrow, would you still resent them? What good would it do? Does the now dead person know that you are still angry with them? No, they wouldn't; so you see, this foolishness. Either way, you still need to love and forgive them so that you yourself can heal and move on. So, as you see, harboring resentment gains you nothing; harboring resentment does not ever "pay the other person back," you are only "paying yourself back" —by poisoning your own body and spirit. Furthermore, when a person chooses to harbor resentment, their resentment often bleeds into other relationships. Therefore, they are likely harming those whom they should otherwise be pouring their love into; such as their children, spouse, family, and friends. The only true antidote for resentment is love, humility, and forgiveness. So you see, God did not give us our own unique gifts and talents for us to use them in unhealthy ways and to use them for our own self-serving reasons so that we could boast pridefully or arrogantly in them. No, He gave them so that we could serve Him and others, and for His glory. If we all had been created with the same talents, gifts, and alike, not only would we altogether be like robots, but it would eliminate our ability to serve one another through love and humility. So, therefore, either we choose to serve out of love and humility and all for the glory of God, or we choose to serve ourselves out of pride, greed, envy, jealousy, resentment, and so on, as we compare and compete with others to our own peril and demise. Therefore, choose love, joy, peace, patience, kindness, goodness, faithfulness, gentleness, and self-control, as you bear fruit for the purpose of honoring God and others in humility.

Colossians 3:12-15

"Put on then, as God's chosen ones, holy and beloved, compassionate hearts, kindness, humility, meekness, and patience, bearing with one another and, if one has a complaint against another, forgiving each other; as the Lord has forgiven you, so you also must forgive. And above all these, put on love, which binds everything together in perfect harmony. And let the peace of Christ rule in your hearts, to which indeed you were called in one body. And be thankful."

CHASING TIME IS LIKE CHASING AFTER THE WIND—YOU WILL NEVER CATCH IT

Ecclesiastes 5:15
"As he came from his mother's womb, naked shall he return, to go as he came; and he shall take nothing from his labor, which he may carry away in his hand."

Hypothetically, let's say you found yourself "stranded" on Earth entirely alone; however, you have access to most of the common luxuries: cars, houses, clothes, various foods, and all other contemporary things, all of which were prefabricated for you upon your arrival. You also have at your disposal the option to live in any size, shape, or style of home you desire and, in your garage, would be the car or cars of your dreams. Still, no one else would ever see the house you live in or the vehicle you drive. Would you be happy and content? The only responsibility you have is to gather food for yourself from the various sources of nature and to maintain and upkeep your necessary possessions in order for you to use them: the house you live in, the car you drive, and so on. How would this affect your choices and decisions in life, knowing that it is only just you? Let's say that you have the means to post to social media; however, everything that you post would, of course, go unseen by anyone. Therefore, you have no reason to impress others, no one to compare to, no one to influence you; you have no need to prove yourself and your worth day after day to anyone. Would you still post? Would you survive without the presence of others who otherwise provide you with attention, validation, justification, and praise—whether it be through physical interaction or through social media? If it were only just you, God the Father, the Son, and the Holy Spirit, and no one else, would you be able to survive through hope, faith, trust, and your relationship with God? How would you spend your time? What if you could share this life with one other person, such as a spouse, partner, friend, etc.? How would this affect your decisions and happiness, and would this one person be enough?

Have you ever wondered or asked yourself, why do I exist in this world and what is my purpose? Well, if you have, you would not be alone. Most every person who has ever lived on the face of Earth will have at some point in their life asked themselves this question. In all reality, it would be worrisome if a person has never questioned the purpose of their existence within this world. Have you ever considered this fact?: That we ourselves did not get to choose whether we wanted to be brought into this world, so why would we then feel that it is our obligation to determine our purpose for being here? Perhaps the answer to this question is truly quite simple, and perhaps we had a purpose before we were ever born into this world. But because we live in a broken and fallen world full of sin and evil, the answer to this question, like many things in life—as they are passed down from generation to generation—becomes lost, distorted, and misconstrued. Oftentimes, our spirit within ("our gut feeling") attempts to warn us when something is not quite right. However, we humans have an overwhelming propensity to ignore these natural (divine) warnings and will live as if everything is "normal" or "okay." We often disregard these warnings because we don't want to face truth and reality; therefore, we instead choose ignorance and deception. We'd rather let our sensualities and emotions lead the way versus truth, logic, and reasoning, because if we were to use logic and reasoning, we then would have to experience grief, sorrow, pain, discomfort, and the truth. I, for most of my childhood, from afar would watch the world function around me, and as I did, I often thought to myself: "Is this really how things are supposed to be?" — "Is this really how we are to be as people?" I often thought as I observed, why were so many people functioning from the same set of rules and acting in the same way, which appeared to be quite robotic and mundane. I would ask myself: "Why do so many people seem to be trying so hard in wanting to be like everyone else and in wanting what everyone else has—all while caring so much about what everyone else thinks?" Things just didn't seem quite right, but I was never sure how to approach all of it, nor did I know what to make of it, aside from the fact that my brain was still developing and maturing. Which, realizing later on in life that many of my questions and much of my thoughts would have made sense had I known about and read the Bible. It wasn't until I was in my mid-20s and upon moving away from where I was raised up, that God began to reveal Himself to me. In that time, I began to discover and uncover the answers to my many questions as a child; as God began to show me the many truths and realities of life. It was then that I began to experience and to realize that it was not God's will for me or anyone else, to be like everyone else; but that I had my own path to walk, a path that God had preemptively laid out for me before bringing me into this world. I also realized that I was not here in this world to work incessantly day in and day out, merely for the sake of "time, money, and success"; just so that I could have what everyone else has. Furthermore, while doing so, sacrificing relationships and my soul (literally) all for the sake of money, power, recognition, validation, and success. Moreover, in the hopes that I could one day "retire." Because never has God commanded, that we are to retire after so many years of work; but to the contrary, He commands us to serve Him and others during our (entire) duration here on earth. Furthermore, just as God has never said that we are to live to work, and that we are to "find our purpose" for our existence while being here. What God does command of us, first and foremost, is that we all are to have a deep and intimate relationship with Him; through love, reverence, and gratitude—glorifying Him throughout our lives each day and in every way—which is the purpose for our existence. God's second command and purpose for us all, is much like the first: which is to be in relation with other people; through His divine love, serving one another and helping each other thrive. And for anyone who is not living for God's purpose, is missing out on the most profound and wondrous meaning of life. Not only are they missing out on their purpose, but they are also missing out on the opportunity to live for eternity with God, in His Kingdom, where everything is perfect, beautiful, wonderful, and utterly fulfilling; and where there is no death, pain, sorrow, or suffering but only the purest peace and love. Therefore, it is imperative to really ponder and consider what God has commanded of us all, and why He commands what He does. I once heard a father say to his son, "You have too much time to think." This statement was said following the son's attempt to share his thoughts and feelings with his father regarding some concerns he had within the family. In some manner, this was a common response from the father anytime the son sought understanding. Now mind you, this father rarely, if ever, spoke about or displayed any sort of deep personal feelings of his own to anyone—at least none that would ever place him in a position of vulnerability or to feel inferior to anyone. Neither did the father ever really give anyone else the time of day if they wanted to present their feelings of concern to him. To this father, feelings or the sharing of feelings were a sign of "weakness," although it was apparent that the father himself was the one who was "weak" and insecure. Therefore, this father's persona of "strength" and "toughness" was to keep his weaknesses, insecurities, and vulnerability, hidden and unseen by others, and from himself nonetheless. This father would rarely, if ever, personally confront anyone on any issues or matters that he may have had with them at the time; not until the matters of concern had festered inside of him for a while, would he then, out of anger, have the "strength" and "confidence" to address his concern, which often led to more uncontrollable anger. For this father, it was more orthodox and "easier" for him to simply just criticize, degrade, and complain to others about the situation than it was for him to approach the person with whom he had the issue. At some point in his life, the father had become so out of touch and disconnected from his innermost self that he couldn't bear the idea of facing someone else's feelings and emotions. Furthermore, because of this disconnection, the father began to display the common characteristics known to society as "multiple personality disorder" or "bipolar." The father, at the flip of a switch, would go from being one person to a completely different person in a matter of seconds, all while having no realization of what was occurring within himself. It was apparent that at some point early on in this father's life, he allowed his heart to become so hardened and numb—to life and himself—that it was his way of forging forward through tough times. What was even more devastating to this man's family was that his wife had also disconnected herself from reality so that she also could just forge ahead in life. Which, as we know, just forging ahead without addressing issues and problems fixes absolutely nothing but only just exacerbates them; thus, leaving only one result—the destruction of people's lives. Sadly, most people often say, "That won't happen to me"; that is until life confronts them, whether they want it to or not. Thus, it isn't until they find themselves buried deep within a situation with no way out that they then take the time to evaluate their life and themselves, but often by this time it is nearly too late. Which is why it is imperative that we all take for ourselves time from every day to do a self-check and to perform a self-evaluation of ourselves and of life overall. If a self-check or evaluation is not occurring at the beginning of our day, then it should certainly be happening at the end of the day. Because if this self-check is not happening at all, soon without knowing, a person will become robotic, instinctive, and habitual, having no control over who they are or of how they act. But will merely be functioning like animals; emulating what the rest of the world is doing without any further thought. Jesus' brother, James, who authored the book of James within the Bible, during one of his teachings was pointing out how there were many people who upon hearing the Word (The Gospel) were not adhering to what was being said. Alluding to the fact that much of what he was teaching was falling on deaf ears. As they would return to their common habitual and evil ways without any attempt to change. He then assimilates this to the person who looks at themselves in the mirror daily without any deep introspection, and as soon as the person walks away from the mirror, they forget what they even look like and who they are:

James 1:23-24

"For if you listen to the word and don't obey, it is like glancing at your face in a mirror. You see yourself, walk away, and forget what you look like."

Certainly, there are many people who do the very thing James describes. They would rather ignore who they are as a person and the evil within their heart by not having to face truth and reality; because truth and reality convicts and opposes their pride and reputation. Thus, they would rather live selfishly in their pride and for their own purposes, than to submit to God. But then there are those who do take time daily to reflect on themselves and on God, and will even do so multiple times throughout the day. However, for many people, this can be difficult, and not because of their lack of attempt, but because their mind is being inundated by many other unwanted thoughts throughout the day. This, in many ways, is not uncommon, especially if you have given your life over to Jesus Christ. Because when you have given your life over to Jesus, you have made the commitment to no longer follow a world that is powered by evil, or even the evil that is in your own heart. Moreover, we also are having to contend with an adversary who not only seeks to destroy us, but wants to also distract us from having this much-needed time with ourselves and with God. This adversary is Satan, and most people don't realize how much of an influence the devil has on our minds and on our ability to focus. This occurs mainly because people would rather ignore the fact that the devil even exists; much like how society ignores the fact that we all were born with evil in our hearts. For most people, this concept is too hard to swallow. Which is precisely what the devil wants; the devil wants everyone to believe that he does not exist, just as much as he wants every human to believe that they themselves are not sinners and that they don't have evil in them. When the devil has a person believing that he does not exist, this is when he can scheme and manipulate undetected, as he tempts and distracts a person with various thoughts and ideas that would otherwise not be their own. Satan, the master manipulator, will use your personal weaknesses to manipulate you in any possible way and will do so for his ultimate goal—which is to destroy you. Satan, the snake that he is, will tempt you with a sinful thought or idea and will do so in the hopes that you will "bite" into it, thus enticing and leading you right into sin. But he doesn't just stop there, because now that you have bitten into the "apple," he will then entice you with shame and guilt, which will often lead you even further into sin:

1 Peter 5:8

"Be sober-minded; be watchful. Your adversary, the devil, prowls around like a roaring lion, seeking someone to devour."

So, you see, the devil wants you to be entirely spiritually

disconnected from God as well as from yourself and others, and will do anything to make it happen. The devil knows his time, and our time here on Earth is limited; therefore, his goal is to take you and anyone else he can with him to his eternal grave (hell). This is why it is so important to take the time every day to check in not only with yourself but with God; to listen, to hear, and to feel for where you are mentally, physically, and spiritually, to affirm that you are where you want to be and that you are on the right path. All too often, people are too prideful and conceited to think that they ever need to check in with themselves or with God because they have "much better" things to do with their time. They perceive the idea of self-reflection as nonsense, as a waste of time; in the idea that it is just some irrelevant practice that only "spiritual" people do. But then there is a practice that many people also perceive to be nonsense, a practice that is even more powerful than the devil himself and is a practice that any person can partake in, which is the power of prayer. Prayer and communication with God is powerful and is the most powerful weapon we have aside from God Himself; therefore, when you pray to God, it is He who will stave off any distracting and unwanted thoughts that you may have. God has the power to intercede and overwhelm those unwanted thoughts, and also has the power to overwhelm the devil himself. But because we humans are fallible and because we live in a world where there is constant spiritual warfare, we can and will struggle with unwanted thoughts and distractions, even while praying to God. However, God understands, He knows what you are going through and what you are up against, just know that He still hears you and knows what you need. We just have to trust in Him; He wants nothing more than for us to have a loving and intimate relationship with Him through daily communication and prayer. Communication with God is as simple as having a conversation with Him, just as you would with anyone else; although many people do struggle with prayer because of their unbelief in prayer and in God. Therefore, prayer must be sincere and intimate; otherwise, you will be doing it in vain. Before discovering prayer and the power of prayer, I myself had practiced meditation; as I would sit quietly for a period of time, detaching myself from any thoughts or even the world around me. Which can and will provide some sense of peace; however, it will not lead you into a personal relationship with God nor will it provide you with deep inner peace that lasts. Oftentimes, people will say that it was through meditation that they came to experience God. However, in all actuality, it wasn't the aspect of meditation that brought them to God; it was more so that God used their quiet time (meditation) to get their attention. The most natural thing for humans to do is to ignore their unwanted or negative thoughts through distractions, which is why self-reflection is so often ignored; because self-reflection challenges people to confront their negative and unwanted thoughts, feelings, and emotions and the root cause of them. Which is why so many people often find themselves functioning purely off other people's emotions and not their own, because facing the root cause of their own would only cause further discomfort. When we keep in touch with ourselves and with God through daily prayer, God in turn draws us near to Him, which is how we stay connected to truth and reality. Staying connected with God is also how we can break free from being overcome by other people's emotions, false realities, and unhealthy patterns. The devil wants us all to believe that we have only one life to live and that this is it. And many people bite into this lie, as they "race against time" in an attempt to experience every possible experience there is to experience here on Earth, all before they die. Even if it means destroying themselves, their relationships, and others in the process. So, ask yourself, are you one who is enslaved to the concept of "capturing time" in the futile attempt to "control time" as you live by the world's "one life to live" ideology? And are you, like many, who are trying to "race against time" just to "make the best of your time" while you can? Then consider this: how can a person capture something that was never meant to be captured? We are not here on Earth to "make the best of OUR time," we are here to make the best of God's time, time that He allots us. By living out our lives for Him, His glory, and for His Kingdom—our eternal home:

Ecclesiastes 3:11

"Yet God has made everything beautiful for its own time. He has planted eternity in the human heart, but even so, people cannot see the whole scope of God's work from beginning to end."

You see, time, as humanity perceives it, is simply and merely just another concept that allows man to believe he is in control. Yet, like many things of this world in which humanity attempts to control, it becomes a concept that ends up producing a negative effect rather than a positive one. How so, you ask? Because, anytime we, you, or I attempt to control something that was never meant to be controlled, in the end, this very thing ends up controlling us. Yet, many people will attempt a go at it, all while completely ignoring the fact that it is a means to no end:

Proverbs 27:1
"Do not boast about tomorrow, for you do not know what a day may bring forth."
Chasing after time or trying to "capture" time is like chasing after the wind—it comes, and it goes; you never know where it begins nor where it stops, you cannot see what comes before it nor do you see what comes after it—it is only the Lord that knows. Now, one might argue that without the concept of time (man-made time, that is), there would be chaos and disorder, and everything would be out of sync. However, let's not forget that before there was ever a clock or technology, humanity functioned off astronomy; but not only off astronomy, but from our own internal clocks, which God has created in each one of us. I think it's safe to say that society functioned more effectively and efficiently during those times. Whereas, what do we see now, chaos and disorder; as humanity endeavors to function based on its own time without God in an unsynchronized and unharmonized world where society attempts to meet never-ending deadlines, where caffeine, anxiety, and sleep deprivation have become the new norm. Thus, humanity and its incorporated concepts of time—for which it has become enslaved too, has created its own god:
Galatians 4:8-10
"Formerly, when you did not know God, you were enslaved to those that by nature are not gods. But now that you have come to know God, or rather to be known by God, how can you turn back again to the weak and worthless elementary principles of the world, whose slaves you want to be once more? You observe days and months and seasons and years!"
Look at nature itself: every living creature (every living organism) —except for humanity—is functioning intrin-

sically and harmoniously as it was meant to. If humanity were to function naturally as it was meant to, there would be a greater quality of life: spiritually, sociologically, psychologically, and physiologically. Evidence has shown that people who stray from working the common 40-50-60-plus hour work weeks are more productive overall while working than those who work inordinate hours. Society's ongoing conventional ideologies of time want us all to believe that "time is of the essence" and that "time is money"; once again, all of which are false realities and facades. One of the greatest lies that relate to the idea of time is the belief that unless a person becomes "successful" in their lifetime or unless they have "made a name for themselves" (aka "leave a legacy"), then it is often said that that person has essentially "wasted" their life and their time under the pretense that they have "failed in life." And as the common adage goes, people will often say: "This or that person was once a "nobody," but now that they have "success" and have become "famous" or have "made a name for themselves" —they are now a "somebody." However, the fact of the matter is this: either everyone here on Earth is a nobody, or everyone here on Earth is somebody; and to God, we are all somebody. Becoming successful, famous, or "leaving a legacy" does not increase or decrease the value or worth of a person. When a person attempts to collaborate time with money—as in "time is money" —this would be the beginning of one's enslavement to time and money, as they "race against time" to procure all that they can of money. Which is why so many people become addicted to the narcotic of "busyness." However, there is also a paradoxical effect that can occur as a result of chasing after time and money, which is procrastination and despair. One might ask, how does procrastination fit into the concept of chasing money and time? I'll tell you: when a person, through many ways, allows themselves to become so wrapped up in their quest to "conquer" time and money, their perceptions and priorities become distorted. And when priorities and perceptions become distorted, truth and reality are left behind. And when truth and reality are no longer the foundation, everything else is built upon a pillar of sand, which eventually crumbles. And the greater the pillar of sand, the greater the fall. It's like the stock market or the housing market; the farther and farther it moves away from truth and reality and into depravation, the harder it will fall. The same goes for relationships; the further a person immerses themselves in money and success, the harder they and their relationships will fall because money and success have become their god. And when everything does crumble because it was built on a pillar of sand, they are crushed under its weight as they wallow in their own self-pity and defeat. Thus, they find themselves caught up in a perpetual cycle of procrastination and devastation as their hopes and dreams have been forever dashed. Which oftentimes is fueled by alcohol, drugs, and many other addictions, as a means to cope and forget. Therefore, they have now found themselves to be in a worse state than that of what they were in before they adhered to the premise of "time is money" —as they attempted to chase after their long-sought-after dreams, and not God. Whereas, if a person was to have put God first in their life and not themselves, they would have otherwise had a solid foundation of truth and reality to stand on, and not a pillar of sand:

Matthew 7:24-27

"Everyone then who hears these words of mine and does them

will be like a wise man who built his house on the rock. And the rain fell, and the floods came, and the winds blew and beat on that house, but it did not fall, because it had been founded on the rock. And everyone who hears these words of mine and does not do them will be like a foolish man who built his house on the sand. And the rain fell, and the floods came, and the winds blew and beat against that house, and it fell, and great was the fall of it."

Therefore, as a person attempts to "conquer" time, money, and success in order to feel validated, respected, or known, they will have at the same time disregarded the fact that they gave up everything of what truly matters in life: God, relationships, and their soul. So you see, humanity has no influence on time itself, nor do we have any ability whatsoever to manipulate it or to control it, and neither do we comprehend it as God comprehends it:

2 Peter 3:8

"But, beloved, be not ignorant of this one thing, that one day is with the Lord a thousand years, and a thousand years as one day."

God Himself owns time; He created it, He controls it, and so therefore it is His. Many people believe that they "deserve" their time here on Earth; as if they created themselves along with the world and the universe. Which is why many people, as they live out their lives, endeavor to control other people and their time. For the majority, as is often depicted through the manner in which they live, will ignore the fact that they will indeed, one day die. We see this common ignorance come to fruition as we hear so often those who make statements such as this: "Only ten more years of work and then I will receive my pension or social security so that I can retire." This line of thinking is most certainly foolish, ignorant, naïve, and even arrogant; who's to say this person will even be alive for another 10 years—much less another day? I say to this person, get real! Tomorrow is not promised, so stop living as if it is and start living for the present, because today may be your last day here on Earth:

James 4:13-14

"Look here, you who say, 'Today or tomorrow we are going to a certain town and will stay there a year. We will do business there and make a profit.' How do you know what your life will be like tomorrow? Your life is like the morning fog—it's here a little while, then it's gone."

Much of what we see today are people living for themselves as they endeavor to live out every possible experience that they can get their hands on so that they can say on their deathbed, "I lived a good life" and "no time was wasted." Which for many of these people the "good life" equated to serving themselves (not others or God) through a life of greed, envy, jealousy, exploitation, hate, theft, lies, and so on. Because here in the "United States of ~~America~~ Consumerism," the agenda is to cram a lifetime's worth of "experiences" into a single day. This ideology leads to destruction and devastation every time; because we are not here on this Earth for our own self-serving reasons for the mere purpose of experiencing every possible experience that there is to experience. Therefore, give up chasing after time as if you are going to catch it, or to keep up with it, or to stay ahead of it, or even to make up for what of it you have lost. But instead, do the opposite of what the world is doing: SLOW DOWN and turn your life over to Jesus Christ and surrender to His time, and to His purpose for your life. So that when your time is up here on Earth, which could be today, you can go be with the Heavenly Father for eternity in His Kingdom—

where there is no "time."

Job 1:21

"And he said, Naked I came from my mother's womb, and naked shall I return. The Lord gave, and the Lord has taken away; blessed be the name of the Lord."

HONORING GOD WITH GRATITUDE IS THE PATH TO FINDING PEACE, JOY, HAPPINESS, AND CONTENTMENT THAT LASTS

Luke 12:16-21

"And he told them a parable, saying, 'The land of a rich man produced plentifully,' and he thought to himself, 'What shall I do, for I have nowhere to store my crops?' And he said, 'I will do this: I will tear down my barns and build larger ones, and there I will store all my grain and my goods. And I will say to my soul, 'Soul, you have ample goods laid up for many years; relax, eat, drink, be merry.' But God said to him, 'Fool!' 'This night your soul is required of you, and the things you have prepared, whose will they be?' So is the one who lays up treasure for himself and is not rich toward God."

There is a common riff that most of us have heard, and it goes something like this: "If I were given a dollar every time so-and-so did this or said that, I would be rich." Well, I will use the same adage in saying this: If I were given a dollar every time I heard someone proclaim that they were not enslaved to or controlled by money, I, myself, would also be rich (with money that is). Though I will admit, there was a time in my life when I also claimed to not be enticed and controlled by money, though I was. I think it is safe to say that money—aside from the idolization of people themselves—sits at the top of the list as being the most idolized object among humans; yet the utter denial of it is profound. For the majority, the enslavement to money is often seen by how it affects their emotions, how they use or spend it, how they hoard it, and how it often dictates their happiness. One of the most conspicuous ways in which one can know whether they are controlled by money is whether they put forth effort into helping others such as the poor and those in need. But also, can they give without hesitation and apprehensiveness, knowing that they will never be repaid for what they give, or do they give with the expectation of receiving something in return? And when they do give, do they give out of guilt and obligation, or do they give because in their heart they truly care? A common phrase (excuse) that is often heard from those who are confronted about their lack of giving will often say something like this: "Well, I work every day, and so that is my contribution and my giving back to the community and society." Oftentimes, it is these very people who also adhere to the ideology that all who are homeless and poor "have brought their circumstances upon themselves," thus they "deserve" the situation they are in. Moreover, you will also find that these very people will also be the ones that adhere to the premise that, "Bad things only happen to "bad" people and good things happen to "good" people." Therefore, they perceive that everything that they themselves have is "rightfully" theirs because they have "earned" it and therefore they "deserve" it. This line of thinking is heartless, narrow-minded, conceited, and just plain foolishness. Any type of attitude where one adheres to the ideology that they "deserve" something is a telltale sign that they have a heart full of conceit and have yet to fully conceptualize what God's grace is and what it even means to be grateful. Moreover, they are unaware of the fact that they, like everyone, deserve nothing; and that all things are merely given by the grace of God. Many of these common ideologies in which so many people have come to live by would be one of many reasons why Jesus throughout Scripture vociferously states in various ways: "How very difficult it will be for the rich to enter the Kingdom of God":

Luke 18:24-25

"How difficult it is for those who have wealth to enter the kingdom of God! For it is easier for a camel to go through the eye of a needle than for a rich person to enter the kingdom of God."

Matthew 19:23-24

"And Jesus said to his disciples, 'Truly, I say to you, only with difficulty will a rich person enter the kingdom of heaven. Again, I tell you, it is easier for a camel to go through the eye of a needle than for a rich person to enter the kingdom of God.'"

You see, there is nothing wrong with having money or even an abundance of it. It is when a person is greedy and ungrateful, and especially when they exploit others for the gain of it, that they get themselves into trouble. I once knew a man who forthrightly proclaimed he was not controlled by money. Yet at the same time, he was exploiting and enabling those whom he knew were struggling with gambling addictions by taking their money. Even more, this same man was also exploiting an elderly man with the intention of gaining his inheritance and was doing so through the means of emotional manipulation and deceit. Portraying to the elderly man that he was there to care for him and to have a relationship with him, when in all reality he was after his inheritance. So, you see, when it comes to money, most people are quick to deceive themselves and others for the gain of it as they completely disregard the reality of what they are doing through their own denial. I also knew of a couple who also proclaimed not to be controlled by money. However, this couple in subtle ways would often in many ways try to depict to others that they were living a life of "financial freedom." This couple would go out and do many adventurous things together, and while doing them, they would make it known to others what they were doing or what they had done for the purpose of their portrayal. Then, one day, this couple's ongoing facade of "financial freedom" became a reality. They had inherited a significant sum of money, which did indeed provide them with "financial freedom" (that is, financial freedom according to conventional societal standards). However, within a short period of obtaining this inheritance, most of the couple's time adventuring together or even just spending time together had slowly dwindled. This was because their otherwise facade of "financial freedom" was no longer an appeal and neither was it necessary. Which further had shown what they were truly living for. Therefore, shortly after receiving the inheritance, the couple became more distant in their marriage as they had come to realize that money and the show of it could not fill the deep, empty void within their hearts. If you are unfamiliar with the common ideology of which conventional society commonly perceives "financial freedom" to be, let me provide you with a quick summation. The common riff goes something like this: "Financial freedom" is when someone has procured enough money to essentially "never run out" or to "live comfortably" during their lifetime, in the idea that they no longer "need" to "worry" about having enough money for their supposed future plans, in whatever that may be. Moreover, in the idea that they have the "freedom" to do essentially whatever they please and to purchase as they please—with no regard to cost. However, let me provide you with my perspective of what it can mean to be "financially free" or what "financial freedom" can look like: financial freedom to me is knowing that God is my security, not money; knowing that God will always provide me with all of what is necessary for me to sustain during my brief time here on Earth. Knowing that I can be content and grateful every single day and in any situation for all that I have, whether it be little or much. But even more, knowing that everything that I already have is the Lord's; and that I am just a steward of what is His. Another perspective of mine concerning what it means to be financially free is this: knowing that all the materialism and money within this world and along with the world itself is slowly passing away. Therefore, in the end, rendering it essentially worthless; in the fact that there is a day coming when every bit of it will be burned up. Knowing that as I live for Christ and not for "financial freedom," I am storing up treasures—treasures that are more valuable than money—for eternity within the Kingdom of God:

Matthew 6:19-20

"Do not lay up for yourselves treasures on earth, where moth and rust destroy and where thieves break in and steal, but lay up for yourselves treasures in heaven, where neither moth nor rust destroys and where thieves do not break in and steal."

Thus, my objective here on Earth is not to obtain "financial freedom," but to maintain my spiritual freedom that I have in Jesus Christ, in knowing that I have an eternal treasure awaiting me in Heaven. Treasures of pure love, joy, peace, and so on; but most of all, God the Father Himself as my ultimate treasure. What we mainly see today are people who endlessly and exhaustively seek from within this world and its bottomless pit of enticements; purpose, success, security, validation, happiness, contentment, and so on—and many will die trying. But even more, many will live for the mere purpose of one day becoming recognized and validated as they endeavor to "leave a legacy" for themselves—just to once again, die trying. The truth of the matter is, despite how hard a person tries, they will never be "enough" predicated upon other people's perspectives, standards, and expectations. Neither will they ever be "enough" based on how much money they have; the amount of success they procure; the amount of education or the number of degrees they receive; by the amount of materialism they have or in what they have; they will never be enough based on how much their family and/or friends love them; they will never be enough based on the number of kids they have; they will never be enough based on how much their children need or love them; and if they are married, not even their spouse can completely fulfill their deepest desires or the deep void within their heart. So, you see, a person will never be "enough" or feel as if they are adequately "enough" so long as they continue to seek purpose and validation from anything or anyone within this world. People and materialism may satisfy a person for a short period, but it will not satisfy them in the long run; because eventually the satisfaction and experience dissipate. And the sooner a person can come to terms with this reality, the sooner their life will begin to change in the most profound ways as they discover that it is only Jesus Christ who can provide everlasting love, joy, peace, validation, security, contentment, and so on. Only Jesus Christ can fill the deep void that every one of us has in our hearts—a deep void that has a very specific shape to it—a shape that was meticulously created by God Himself. Thus, it is only God who can fit into this shape, and He intended it to be this way. Yet, most people will attempt to fit, stuff, shove, and force just about anything and everything and anyone they possibly can into this void, just to fill it. And because we live in a world where the premise of autonomy and self-preservation has become first priority—as the majority chase after their "dreams" and "aspirations," the implications of this catastrophic ideology are devastating—as relationships and mental health take the brunt of it. Moreover, while societal conventional "wisdom" further teaches and reinforces this ideology, it insinuates that if a person has not accomplished their "dreams" or "aspirations" and has not "made a name for themselves" during their time here on Earth, this person is deemed a failure. But not only are they now a failure, they are also a "nobody," —says conventional "wisdom." This ongoing premise is of course nothing more than one cataclysmic lie, yet most of the world continues to adhere to it. I, for a good part of my life, also adhered to this lie; but thanks be to God and His grace, for opening my eyes and ears to the truth and reality of it all. Unless you have been living in a cave most of your life, we have all seen or have heard the many stories and accounts of people who have achieved their "aspirations," "dreams," and "goals." Yet despite their "success," they found themselves to be miserable and empty inside. Moreover, even upon their "success," these very same people often find themselves to be in more of a miserable state than that of what they were in before they obtained their "success." This occurs because despite their "success," they are now having to face the truth and reality of who they are as a person, the life they are living, and the lies the world has fed them.

Which is why so many people, despite their "success," end up turning to drugs, alcohol, sex, and other addictions in order to numb and cope. Because once again, there is only one source from which complete and everlasting contentment can ever be derived, and that derivative is Jesus Christ. Therefore, if the Creator of our existence is not first in a person's life—though that person may be alive physically here on Earth—that person is perishing spiritually because they search for security, contentment, purpose, validation, love, etc., in all the wrong places. If you find yourself asking, "How is a person passing away spiritually within this world if they are still alive?" Well, let me explain to help you better understand; as I myself did not understand for many years, and was once dead: Hypothetically, let's say that you are living your life as if God essentially does not exist, whether it be through complete rejection of Him or that you are just not living wholeheartedly in relation with Him but instead are living mainly for this world and all that it has to offer. Either way, you are not ultimately living for God and in relation with Him, therefore, your spirit (your soul) is perishing because you do not have the Spirit of eternal life (The Holy Spirit—God) residing within you. Thus, just as the world is passing away—you also are passing away right along with it. In the passage you are about to read, Jesus further clarifies this—as these very words were spoken by Him, stating that you can either live for the world and die with the world, or you can live for God and with God, for eternity:

John 12:25-26

"Whoever loves his life loses it, and whoever hates his life in this world will keep it for eternal life. If anyone serves me, he must follow me; and where I am, there will my servant be

also. If anyone serves me, the Father will honor him."
In the passage you just read, the word love is being used to describe a person who loves themselves and this world more than anything or anyone else, and does so in a selfish and conceited manner. Therefore, they love themselves and the things of this world more than God Himself. In this same passage, the context in which the word hate is being used, does not mean that a person should literally hate themselves. It's saying that in comparison to the love that you should have for God, in contrast, would look like hate for yourself and the world. Think of it this way: though you do love yourself (in a healthy manner and not in conceitedness) and others, your love for yourself and others should hold no comparison to how much you love God. We all have a deep need within our hearts for love, just as we all have a deep longing for a permanent home; however, we must first come to terms with the fact that this world is not it and stop living as if it is. Therefore, until a person can fully accept this truth, they will endeavor endlessly to find love, joy, peace, happiness, comfort, security, purpose, validation, and contentment, all of which can only be found in Jesus Christ and in His Kingdom. We were all created by God out of His pure love in the idea that we all are to have an intimate and loving relationship with Him first and foremost; living to worship Him and glorify Him with gratitude is the reason for humanity's existence here on Earth. But then we also are to serve Him and others through His love while being in relationship with others. You see, we were not placed here on Earth to first serve ourselves by living for ourselves; we are here to serve others through serving God first. Don't miss the importance of that last sentence and the way in which I stated it—God first, then others. If you at-

tempt to serve others first and not God first, then you are likely serving out of obligation and not from a place of love, and are doing so as a means to gain praise for yourself and to essentially "score points" with God—endeavoring to "earn" your salvation as you attempt to "work" your way into Heaven. Which, by the way, is impossible; furthermore, if you are doing this, then you are serving yourself first, and not God first. Whereas, if you serve God first, you will then out of love for others (and not obligation) want to serve others. It's the same concept of why a person should want to give and to help those in need, such as the impoverished; thus, they give to the impoverished not out of obligation and guilt but because they love the impoverished and want to truly help. Moreover, if a person is serving and giving from a place of guilt or obligation, then they are essentially seeking a reward in the idea that God "owes" them something for their "work" or for what they have done. Thus, they are once again back to serving themselves and not God, as they attempt to "earn" their salvation in the idea that they "deserve" their salvation—or anything else that they might have. Moreover, to take it a step further as it were, they are essentially attempting to manipulate God in their attempt to "earn" their salvation based on merit. Yes, that is manipulation, so don't deceive yourself in the idea that it is not. A prime example of this would be the many parents who will attempt to manipulate and "buy" their way into the hearts of their children by lavishing upon them money and materialism, in the idea that their children will "love" them more because of it. If you are a Christian of the Gospel, then you know that a person—cannot—in any way— "earn" their salvation nor can they "work" their way into heaven based on anything they do or don't do. But that a person can only enter into the Kingdom of God through faith in Jesus Christ by accepting God's Grace; that, which is Jesus Christ. Thus, you are saved by Grace (Jesus Christ) and not by "works." And though faith is dead without works, a Christian works not because it saves them, but because they are saved by Grace (Jesus). Therefore, they work to serve God first, and then others, and not themselves:

1 Peter 4:10

"As each has received a gift, use it to serve one another, as good stewards of God's varied grace."

You should now be seeing the connection here. EVERYTHING revolves around God, not us. Thus, be very cautious about your motives for wanting to serve or to give; or you will end up not only hurting yourself but you will also be hurting the very people who you are supposed to be helping and serving (out of love). Here is an example of what I mean when I say you will end up hurting those of whom you are wrongfully serving: Let's take a look at a mother who loves her child selfishly versus a mother who loves her child selflessly. First, let's start with the selfless mother who loves and cares for her child in every possible way and does so for the best interest of the child, short-term and long-term. This caring and loving mother has a child who wants to go outside to the playground; the child wants to explore, experience, and wants to meet new friends. Thus, the mother encourages the child to go because the mother knows it will be good for the child in the sense that the child will become better equipped for life overall as they in various ways grow, even into adulthood. The mother knows that if she is overprotective of the child, the child will never learn how to deal and cope with significant problems such as how to protect themselves from threats and exploitation and will not have the confidence nor the wherewithal to do so. Now, let's look at the mother who selfishly "loves" her child: This mother does many things for the child but does them in the interest of herself and not for the best interest of her child. This mother, like the last, also has a child who wants to go outside to play and to interact with the world; however, this mother through control and manipulation hinders the child from going out to play because she herself thrives off the attention that her child provides her. And because her child is what validates her existence and her purpose for living life here on Earth. Within these two scenarios, you see the contrast of the two mothers; one mother is seeking to serve herself, while the other is seeking to serve God and her child. Self-serving becomes a vicious cycle that occurs in the lives of so many, whether it be in a parent-child relationship, a spousal relationship, a sibling relationship, a vocational relationship, or any other relationship. Only a transformed heart through a relationship with Jesus Christ can break a person free from their perpetual self-serving madness. The ultimate covenant of God is that if we turn away from sin and accept Christ Jesus as our Lord and Savior by believing in Him with all our heart, soul, mind, and strength, then we are to become His children. However, we have a choice in the matter; if we choose to live for ourselves and in our own ways, then that is what God allows us to do. God is not going to force us into anything; He never does and never will. However, this is not to say that when we do choose our own way in lieu of God's way, that He isn't going to try to nudge, compel, correct, or redirect us back to Him. Therefore, when a person chooses Jesus and to walk within His Light, their inner darkness (evil) slowly fades away while

their heart and soul are being transformed; this would be the rebirthing process of a Christian and is what it means to be born again. Thus, through Jesus Christ, you become a vessel of the Light and a child of the Most-High God:
John 1:9-13
"The true light, which gives light to everyone, was coming into the world. He was in the world, and the world was made through him, yet the world did not know him. He came to his own, and his own people did not receive him. But to all who did receive him, who believed in his name, he gave the right to become children of God, who were born, not of blood nor of the will of the flesh nor of the will of man, but of God."
1 John 3:1-10
"See what kind of love the Father has given to us, that we should be called children of God; and so, we are. The reason why the world does not know us is that it did not know him. Beloved, we are God's children now, and what we will be has not yet appeared; but we know that when he appears we shall be like him, because we shall see him as he is. And everyone who thus hopes in him purifies himself as he is pure. Everyone who makes a practice of sinning also practices lawlessness; sin is lawlessness. You know that he appeared in order to take away sins, and in him there is no sin. No one who abides in him keeps on sinning; no one who keeps on sinning has either seen him or known him. Little children, let no one deceive you. Whoever practices righteousness is righteous, as he is righteous. Whoever makes a practice of sinning is of the devil, for the devil has been sinning from the beginning. The reason the Son of God appeared was to destroy the works of the devil. No one born of God makes a practice of sinning, for God's seed abides in him; and he cannot keep on sinning, because he has been born of God. By this it is evident who are the children of God, and who are the children of the devil: whoever does not

practice righteousness is not of God, nor is the one who does not love his brother."

God commands us to be confident and bold in our faith, trusting in who Jesus is and what He has done for us. God tells us to be confident and bold in our love, mercy, and grace towards others and toward this world. God tells us to be bold and confident in humility, despite knowing that we will be taken advantage of, criticized, and ridiculed, just as Jesus was—even to the point of death. As children of God, God knows that much of what happened to His Son Jesus can and will happen to us. And though we may be persecuted in all the same ways Jesus was, God is a just God and will without doubt indemnify every wrongdoing that occurs:

Romans 12:19-21

"Beloved, never avenge yourselves, but leave it to the wrath of God, for it is written, 'Vengeance is mine, I will repay, says the Lord.' To the contrary, 'if your enemy is hungry, feed him; if he is thirsty, give him something to drink; for by so doing, you will heap burning coals on his head.' Do not be overcome by evil, but overcome evil with good."

Deuteronomy 7:9-14

"Know therefore that the LORD your God is God, the faithful God who keeps covenant and steadfast love with those who love him and keep his commandments, to a thousand generations, and repays to their face those who hate him, by destroying them. He will not be slack with one who hates him. He will repay him to his face. You shall therefore be careful to do the commandment and the statutes and the rules that I command you today. And because you listen to these rules and keep and do them, the LORD your God will keep with you the covenant and the steadfast love that he swore to your fathers. He will love you, bless you, and multiply you. He

will also bless the fruit of your womb and the fruit of your ground, your grain and your wine and your oil, the increase of your herds and the young of your flock, in the land that he swore to your fathers to give you. You shall be blessed above all peoples. There shall not be male or female barren among you or among your livestock."

Therefore, be content and grateful for what God has already given you, and He may even bless you with more —or He may not—it is His choice—He knows best—so either way, be grateful. That said, don't fall prey to the common ideology and deception that just because you have many materialistic things or even non-materialistic things such as good health, that you deserve or have earned any of it. Because, you can know for certain, as the same goes for every one of us, we do not deserve anything we have and that everything we do have, is given purely by God's grace. The only thing each of us deserves, is death on a cross, which our Lord and Savior Jesus Christ took for us. The moment a person begins to believe that they deserve or are entitled to anything, is a good indication that they not only are on the wrong path but are completely undermining God:

James 1:7-11

"For a person must not suppose that he will receive anything from the Lord; he is a double-minded man, unstable in all his ways. Let the lowly brother boast in his exaltation, and the rich in his humiliation, because like a flower of the grass he will pass away. For the sun rises with its scorching heat and withers the grass; its flower falls, and its beauty perishes. So also, will the rich man fade away in the midst of his pursuits."

Many people give their lives over to eternal death just so they can live in "comfort" or luxury for the present moment. Moreover, through deceit and denial, many people will disregard the truth and reality that they will one day die and that their time here on Earth is really quite brief. Therefore, in their denial, they chase after the short-lived comforts, pleasures, false securities such as success and money, to only then forfeit their soul in the end. Most people will spend their entire lives living and working within the same environment and will do so not because they are truly content or happy, but because they have become enslaved to its "comforts" and "securities." And though they may even be miserable with where they are, they will continue living where they have been for so long just so they can maintain their feeling of being in "control." Which is why when anything goes wrong, such as the loss of their career or home, they are utterly devastated. Because, for so long, they have been putting their trust in those things; such as their career, money, materialism, and not God. You see, comfort does not equate to happiness, nor does comfort come from living within your own "comfortably" "controlled" environment. Oftentimes, a person through excuse upon excuse will tell themselves that they are essentially "stuck" with where they are and with no way out, when in all reality, they are afraid to give up control and have faith in God. Which by doing so, it often leads them down a path of perpetual bitterness and resentment as they begin to blame everyone and everything for their current situation. Moreover, many of these same people will choose to continue living within the same location and area of where they were born and raised. And if they do leave, they oftentimes find their way back because it's familiar territory: near family, friends, and other relatives. Oftentimes, people will say that they "stay close to home so that they can be near family and friends," but in all reality, it is for their own self-serving reasons for which they will never admit. Because where there is family and friends, there is "convenience," "comfort," "security," resources that are already in place—especially for a couple who is planning to have children. However, even then, after moving "back home," they eventually find themselves "stuck" and unhappy again because their quest to "be closer to family" didn't meet their preconceived notions and expectations. Thus, their expectations of "Living the American Dream" didn't go as planned—as their deepest desires were not fulfilled. So now, they are back to having to face the realities of life in the fact that nothing within this world will satisfy them for the long run. But then it doesn't just end there; oftentimes, people will then revert to the premise of living a life vicariously through others. Which is all too common nowadays with having social media and television at our fingertips 24/7. Thus, as a person succumbs to the addiction of scrolling and watching, it allows people to follow and watch others incessantly and obsessively as they numb themselves from their own reality. Oftentimes, people will begin to idolize those whom they follow on social media or television and will begin to mirror their actions and even the life they are living as they endeavor to find their identity through that person. A prime example of this would be the idolization of a sports team or even a team member; as we often see adult men and women walking around with clothing that has other people's names and numbers on it. Or the many men and women who follow and watch various types of celebrities in their attempt to—in every possible way—be like them in their idolization of them. However, most people won't admit to their idolization and obsession and will attenuate the reality of it by claiming that what they are doing is being done in "fun" or in "support" of that person. So not only do they idolize this person or persons whom they are incessantly following on social media or elsewhere, but they begin to psychologically worship this person—as their idol becomes their god. This worshiping and idolization doesn't just start or stop with people; it's in every realm of life; even animals such as dogs have become idols and have become way more than just "man's best friend." They've become people's identity. We live in a world where animals such as dogs are being pampered and prioritized over feeding and sheltering the poor and homeless. The primary reason behind why one human will idolize and worship another, or anything else for that matter, is because they are spiritually lost and are trying to find something or someone to fill that deep, empty void within their soul. The deep and empty void that only Jesus Christ can fulfill. Most often, it is a child's upbringing that leaves a person without any form of identity because they were not raised up in knowing and having a relationship with God. Therefore, they search perpetually for someone to model after, even as an adult. Which is why careers and success are the most predominant sought-after forms of validation and identification. Therefore, if you, like many, seek to find your identity and purpose from the things within this world, you have already taken the first step down the arduous path to long-term discontentment. People will often say to themselves, "If only I had this one thing, then I would be happy," or "If only I had one more of these, then I would be happy," or "If I buy this house," or "If I buy this car," or "If only I had this piece of land or property," or "If only I had this scenic view," or "If only I was married or in a relationship," or "If only I had a child or if we have this many children," or "If only I had this degree or education," or "If only I had this career," then I will be happy and content. So, you see how this becomes a perpetual cycle that never ends, yet almost everyone does it. A very well-known example of this, which many of us can relate to, was the purchase of our first car and how excited we were once we obtained it. The car quickly became our idol as the car essentially became our new "home away from home" and our freedom: cleaning and washing it every week and buying new things to add or to put into it. However, eventually reality started to set in, and within a short period of time, our emotional highs of owning the car started to dwindle; the endorphins (the feel-good chemicals) within our brain were no longer being released as they once were upon the initial thought of purchasing and owning this grand car. Therefore, after a period of time, we then find ourselves back to point A; feeling discontent, just as we were before the idea of purchasing a car had ever come to fruition. Not only are we now back to point A, feeling discontent and unhappy, but are now irritated and maybe even resentful because now the car has become a burden. The car is costing us money, time, and even our happiness because now we are having to give more of our time to our job just to pay the expense of owning the car. Moreover, we are now in over our heads in debt because we paid more than we should have for the car; because we let our emotions dictate how much we should spend on the car to begin with versus thinking through it logically and rationally. This common car scenario can be applied to just about every other aspect of life when it comes to decision-making, where our emotions and feelings often become our guide. Which, by the way, car dealerships—especially salesmen—thrive on this concept. What is most astonishing about this very situation, like many others, is how quickly we humans have the propensity to forget what we had learned through previous experiences. Thus, we so often will repeat our hard-learned actions by going back, just to do it all over again. Which, truth be told, is often an indication that we lack gratitude for what we already have as one continues to search the things of this world for fulfillment. Because if we were truly grateful for what we already have, we wouldn't continue to allow our emotions and feelings to dictate our actions in the expectation that another "new shiny toy" is going to bring us happiness, peace, joy, and contentment. Now, I can hear someone saying, "Well, that's just life and is the way things go." My response to them would be this: no, it is not "just life and the way things go," it is foolishness and is what conventional society teaches and enables people through its enticement of consumerism, materialism, and the man-made luxuries of this world. And is all the more reason why people need Jesus, and not materialism. Which, truth be told, you cannot serve the desires of your flesh and God at the same time—it's either one or the other:

Luke 16:13

"No servant can serve two masters, for either he will hate the one and love the other, or he will be devoted to the one and despise the other. You cannot serve God and money."

A telltale sign that someone is unhappy with themselves or with where they are in life is when you experience a person who is often negatively involved, gossiping and meddling in other people's affairs, unprovoked. They often feel the need and will attempt to bring others down into their world of darkness and misery just to make themselves feel better. We all have our struggles, but overall if a person is truly grateful and content as they walk in relation with Jesus Christ, they naturally will find themselves wanting to encourage and build others up versus always attempting to destroy and tear others down. Yet, many people choose to forgo God and to forgo all that He has to offer because they are too proud to give up control and to give up their own ways of thinking. Therefore, they live a life full of lies and false realities just so they don't have to confront themselves in who they are and the life they are living. They'd rather complain, covet, compare, hate, judge, envy, and live in denial than to make changes in their own life and to stop blaming "the world" for their problems. The only way to find long-lasting peace, joy, happiness, and contentment during your time here on Earth is by showing endless gratitude towards Jesus Christ and what He has done for you on the cross and for what He has already given you in this present time. Thus, are you breathing right now? Wonderful, be content and grateful; show it by giving your life over to Jesus Christ and His Kingdom, where you will have everlasting peace, joy, happiness, and contentment, right along with His unconditional and incomprehensible love. Remember, God breathed life into your lungs, so worship and glorify Him with your lungs, each day and all day, with gratitude and love.

Genesis 2:7

Then the LORD God formed the man from the dust of the ground. He breathed the breath of life into the man's nostrils, and the man became a living person.

Matthew 6:33-34

"But seek first the kingdom of God and his righteousness, and all these things will be added to you. Therefore, do not be anxious about tomorrow, for tomorrow will be anxious for itself.

Sufficient for the day is its own trouble."

ACKNOWLEDGEMENT

All Glory Be To God

www.ingramcontent.com/pod-product-compliance
Lightning Source LLC
LaVergne TN
LVHW090519110826
845146LV00003B/916

* 9 7 9 8 9 9 4 8 1 8 9 4 7 *